Introducing
Total Quality Management
A Credit Union Reader

Produced in Cooperation with Your
Credit Union League and CUNA & Affiliates

Product #20322

KENDALL/HUNT PUBLISHING COMPANY
4050 Westmark Drive P.O. Box 1840 Dubuque, Iowa 52004-1840

CONTENTS

"SNAPSHOTS" OF QUALITY

SELECTED ARTICLES

- "Principles of Total Quality," *Modern Office Technology,* February 1992.

- "Deming's 14 Points Applied to Service," *Training,* March 1991.

- "How to Improve Quality if You're NOT in Manufacturing," *Training,* November 1992.

- "Just What, Exactly, Is Quality Service?" *ABA Banking Journal,* June 1992.

- "Quality Coaches: A Look at Their Game Plans for Turning Firms into Winners," *CPI Purchasing Magazine,* March 1986.

- "Special Report: Credit Unions Focusing on Quality," *Credit Union Manager Newsletter,* April 1993.

- "How to Get Your TQM Training on Track," *Nation's Business,* October 1992.

- "Training for TQM: Pulling Together for the 'Quality Journey'," *Credit Union Magazine,* May 1993.

- "The Infrastructure for Total Quality Management," *TQM Magazine,* November–December 1993.

ILLUSTRATIONS

PURPOSE OF THIS HANDBOOK

This handbook provides basic information for anyone interested in exploring and applying Total Quality Management (TQM) concepts, methods, and tools within a credit union environment. If TQM is going to be more than the latest addition to a list of outdated phrases, it must work for all businesses, withstand the test of time, and most importantly, produce lasting results.

This book accepts one of the major premises of TQM—that the nature of business is changing. No business exists in a vacuum. To thrive in the coming century, credit unions must quickly adapt to member demands and an ever-changing environment. TQM offers a system for survival.

TQM is not a quick-fix solution for a troubled company. It is based on the premise that success follows from a continual process of change and improvement. Likewise, quality improvement is a process of evolution requiring long-term commitment.

Use this handbook as a quality "primer." It introduces the major TQM principles and concepts and TQM's leading theorists. And it goes one step further than a mere "primer." This handbook explores how TQM works in the credit union. Traditionally, TQM focuses on the manufacturing industry. The service industry, however, also meets real consumer needs, though its products are not always tangible and are generally brought to market in a different manner.

This handbook considers how credit unions around the country use TQM. What works? What doesn't? It offers a starting point and can help you in the following ways:

- Give you an overview of the vast amount of information about TQM.
- Demonstrate that TQM is an integrated management system—not a quick-fix solution.
- Show you how your peers in the credit union movement have applied TQM concepts.

Also included is a selection of articles reprinted from various publications. They will help to supplement the text, and they focus on credit unions and the service sector.

Finally, please take a moment to fill out the evaluation form found on page 135.

WHAT IS QUALITY?

"...You can talk about quality, but if you don't know what to do about it, bring it about, quality is an empty word."

W. Edwards Deming[1]

Quality. Your members not only want it, they expect it. Credit unions everywhere are competing to make sure their products and services bear the mark of quality their members want. But where does a manager start? How does management know it's leading the credit union in the right direction?

First, management must define quality. What does it mean to members? What does it mean to employees?

The standard Webster's Dictionary entry defines quality as a "peculiar and essential character, a distinguishing attribute." Standard business school textbooks offer definitions such as "quality is the value of the goods and services as perceived by the customer." Many companies emphasize quality to restore America's competitive edge. They are looking for a way to increase productivity, lower costs, and promote greater customer satisfaction. Quality assurance programs, quality member service, and quality circles help focus attention on the value of products and services. In fact, quality control now commands its own entry in the dictionary.

Credit unions enjoy a history of attention to members and their needs. Credit union values align in many ways with the intended by-products of quality. For example, credit unions are known for their commitment to:

- Good member service – Credit unions were founded to serve and help members.

- Low interest rates – Credit unions were established to offer low-interest loans to working people.

- Teamwork – Cooperation and mutual trust form the foundation of the credit union philosophy.

---

[1] As quoted by Mary Walton, from her account of a Feb. 5–8, 1985 Deming seminar. *The Deming Management Method,* (New York: Putnam Books, 1986), 26.

All quality initiatives can potentially bring a credit union closer to the goal of achieving total quality. But Total Quality Management is not just a handshake and a smile, a quality circle, or a new computer program to speed transaction time. By themselves, these well-intentioned initiatives constitute only a single element of an entire quality program. An increasing volume of research suggests that, by itself, a single, quality initiative will not ensure quality throughout an organization. For instance, improvements in transaction time at the teller window may please your members momentarily, but a single improvement will not ensure ongoing member satisfaction if other services throughout the credit union fail to provide the degree of quality members expect.

Perhaps your credit union already emphasizes quality in all aspects of its operations. But in many credit unions, even the best intentions fall short. Management's search for the ultimate quality initiative is like the old-world explorers' quest for the fountain of youth—they never found the magical fountain for which they searched. So it is with quality. Quality may be easily visualized, but not easily achieved. We will never find a single, easy method for maintaining quality.

So how can credit unions make sure that every transaction fulfills member expectations? Unfortunately, managers will not find a single, simple answer. But they will find a direction through Total Quality Management.

TQM: WHAT IS IT AND WHAT DOES IT MEAN?

Total Quality Management, as the name suggests, offers an all-encompassing view of achieving quality and long-term organizational viability. The TQM philosophy puts quality at the foundation of the company. It emphasizes that every part of an organization works together and must be involved in a quality effort characterized by meeting and exceeding customers' expectations.

TQM is an approach to managing a business. It is not a magical overnight formula for achieving quality. Rather, managers in search of quality will find that TQM is an approach to management that requires companies to define their mission, determine how they will help employees deliver quality products and services, and establish plans for achieving ongoing quality management as a strategic organizational objective. But above all, TQM puts the credit union member at the center of all decisions.

One essential component of TQM is strategic planning. By using strategic planning, an organization can design an implementation route for reaching its goals.

A TQM Success Story: Baxter Credit Union

Baxter Credit Union in Deerfield, Illinois, has been successfully practicing TQM for the past four years. Because of TQM, Baxter CU is 85–90% loaned out, has a delinquency rate of less than .2%, has a 5% employee turnover rate, was the only service division to win the 1992–1993 Baxter Corporation's quality award, and has 30 credit unions benchmarking against it. So what can we learn from Baxter CU?

Employee Rewards

Rex Johnson, President and CEO at Baxter CU, firmly believes in giving incentives to employees. "It's extra work for an employee to process fifteen loans a week rather than five. If you believe you shouldn't be giving rewards for good performance because offering and processing loans 'is their job,' then you should be satisfied that your employees are just meeting the requirements. And if their job descriptions say 'five loans

(continued)

a week,' why should employees work harder and put up with the hassle to process fifteen?"

All employees, from marketing to collection to phone center to back office, are able to earn bonuses based on performance. This way, employees are able to control how much they earn.

Rex explains why he believes in individual incentives and not team incentives. "Two things I learned while getting my master's at Northwestern were 'never fail to reward employees for good performance' and 'never reward poor performance.' In my opinion, team incentives can reward low producers. They reward high achievers that work doubly hard to pick up the slack of the rest of the team as well as the low producer that knows he or she can ride the coattails of the others."

Employee Empowerment

All Baxter CU employees are empowered to waive up to $100 in charges or fees without approval. "This leads to good member service," Rex said. "For example, a member who always pays her VISA balance monthly has a late payment. She calls Baxter CU to explain that it was the post office's mistake. The employee can immediately waive the fee without inconveniencing the member at all. So the member isn't left feeling frustrated or embarrassed, and the employee doesn't feel helpless to provide good service. We give our staff the resources to do whatever it takes to make sure the member gets what he or she is asking for."

Employee Training

Baxter CU believes that employees need training to do their jobs well. All new tellers spend the first two weeks in training at a training center equipped with mock teller stations and computer terminals. As well as learning about their jobs, they'll learn cross-selling, transactions, and credit union philosophy.

Baxter CU takes its commitment to quality and employee training so seriously that it includes quality training in every employees' job description. Employees spend two hours a week for the first fourteen weeks in quality training. At the end of the session, employees sign a Quality Policy. "Why do employees sign a Quality Policy? Because when employees sign their name to something, they feel a sense of ownership," Rex said.

Management's Commitment

It's imperative to have 100% manager commitment for TQM to work. At Baxter CU, management is visibly committed. For example, at all times, a senior manager is available to assist and approve loans. During rush hours—between 11 and 1 and between 4 and 5—all senior managers are required to be on the floor to help process loans. Members can actually see Baxter CU's commitment to quality and service.

As well as teaching the employee quality training sessions, the four vice-presidents each head a quality team which meets once a month. The vice-presidents also meet with every

> *manager in all the branches once every two months to discuss what's happening in the manager's department. This gives the managers a chance to discuss any accomplishments, as well as try out any new ideas. Managers are able to receive instant approval on any new ideas. "If management isn't completely committed to TQM, then it will never work. If we don't walk the talk, why should the rest of the staff?" said Rex.*

Strategic planning provides direction to the company by putting long- and medium-range company goals into action. Also known as "*hoshin* planning" in Japan, strategic planning puts the "total" in Total Quality Management.

Another basic tenet of TQM is a commitment to continuous improvement. This commitment is vital, because products and services will never reach perfection, since they must undergo constant improvement to keep pace with changes in the marketplace. Changes could involve member needs or expectations, government regulations, technological advances, and economic fluctuations. This disposition allows credit unions to respond to external influences and continue to succeed. Continuous improvement affects every aspect of an organization because there is always room for improvement. And it involves every person—directors of the board, managers, and workers alike. In Japan, they call this concept *Kaizen*—meaning continuous, never-ending improvement.

For U.S. businesses to regain the strength and respect they once enjoyed, they must find a new way to serve customers. Proponents of TQM offer an approach to a company's management that puts quality at the center of every internal and external process. At credit unions, for example, TQM would pervade every process—each member contact, report, meeting, decision, and performance appraisal.

No definitive school of thought represents TQM. Numerous theorists and consultants offer TQM models. However, Mark P. Finster, University of Wisconsin professor of business, suggests that all TQM initiatives share some common elements—philosophy, systems, methods, tools, and applications.

PHILOSOPHY (PRINCIPLES)

A TQM system is based on a philosophy, a set of principles that form the foundation on which a company builds its transformation. Some companies may call these principles values. These principles or values guide all decisions, strategic plans, and operations, and therefore will be defined early in the TQM process. Since each business defines its customers and their expectations differently, the principles also will differ for every company. A principle might be a statement such as:

- "We'll always put member needs above our own."

- "We value integrity."

- "Employee participation and creativity are the backbone of our business."

SYSTEMS

According to Finster, TQM is a system that consists of three interdependent components: strategic management, daily management, and cross-functional management. Managers can direct their quality transformation by focusing on the operation of each of these components. Finster explains this system through an illustration with three circles linked together, each serving as a key component of the company. This diagram is called the Total Quality Control Circle.

System Components

Figure 1. **Total Quality Control Circle**

Strategic Management

One circle includes strategic, or policy management, which is the part of the business that is led by senior management and engages every part of the organization to achieve major breakthroughs. This is where the quality transformation is initiated and draws its strength and momentum. It includes the planning that helps the TQ transformation maintain long-term viability.

Strategic management includes four phases:

- Conduct analysis/formulate the strategy

- Develop plan

- Engage minds and input of all workers to include action plan

- Implement plan and check progress through periodic review

Daily Management

The second circle includes daily management, where employees take control of their jobs and managers work with them to help improve their environment. Daily management requires empowering employees so they can use their creativity to improve products and processes. It focuses on the needs of each customer or member group, including internal customers or business partners.

The daily management component of the TQM system requires that managers help employees maintain a sense of ownership and pride in their work. Managers must initiate the commitment to quality, stand by it, and provide the resources, recognition, policies, training, and coaching to nurture it. TQM puts decision-making power in the hands of employees. It gives employees and members a voice.

Under the traditional, autocratic style of management, managers or supervisors simply made a decree and expected employees to fall in line. But the autocratic style of management undermines employees' potential to contribute to improvement. It actually encourages employees not to think. It often strips an employee of self-esteem and enthusiasm.

Autocratic management can also translate to frustration for the member. Managers who have little contact with employees may not understand the basic processes of a job; they understand member needs and expectations even less. Without input from the "front-line," management cannot make informed decisions. Members become frustrated if their expressed needs are not met. They're also frustrated when they are made to wait for a simple solution. Employees with no authority or accountability cannot serve members' special needs. Instead, they have to find a supervisor to correct a problem or make even the slightest accommodation.

On the other hand, TQM uses a positive, self-directed approach to manage-

Improving Member Service

At **Citizens Equity Federal Credit Union** in Peoria, Illinois, employees know they can make on-the-spot decisions without seeking management approval. In one instance, a member's money accidentally blew away at the drive-up window. The teller decided to replace the lost bills on the spot. The employee's ability to restore the money without keeping the member waiting demonstrated the credit union's commitment to its members.

In another instance, CEFCU Quality Circle chose to evaluate the amount of cash which could be returned to the member without management approval. This group of employees from all organizational levels discovered a great deal of time was spent obtaining approvals for cash back to the member. In most cases, the higher amount was approved. The process improvement team determined a higher level of empowerment was appropriate and requested a higher limit on the amount of cash a Member Assistant could return to the member without a manager's approval. The initiative and in-depth research presented to the management team gained acceptance of this project. Now CEFCU's Member Assistants use their good judgment and experience in conjunction with guidelines to decide when to exceed cash back limits. Terry Lake, CEFCU's Human Resource Development Manager, says this change saves time and money, improves employee self-esteem, and, most importantly, provides quality member service.

ment. Managers must commit to building a foundation based on quality principles. However, they recognize that a successful quality transformation depends on educating employees and empowering them to make decisions. That, in turn, improves the quality of services. Under TQM, managers and supervisors encourage employees to ask "Why?" before blindly following leaders' orders. Empowerment advocates that employees make suggestions, and it rewards them for improving processes.

In order to make this style of management work in your credit union, it is imperative that you have board of directors' buy-in. You can accomplish this through education and communication. Communicate early and often.

Cross-Functional Management

The third circle of business components that managers must consider in their TQM transformation includes cross-functional management, the interaction that happens between different parts of the system (including suppliers and customers) to support the whole. Teamwork serves as a key element of cross-functional management. It's the opposite of one department not knowing what the others are doing—or departments only speaking to each other through the proper channels.

For example, when the item processing department fails to start payroll deduction on time, it can cause a member's loan to become delinquent. This creates a

Empower Your Employees

Many credit unions are realizing that the key to quality service is employee empowerment. **State Capitol Employees Credit Union** *in Madison, Wisconsin, believes that employees must be given a certain amount of authority in order to offer first-class service to their members. Employees are empowered to:*

- *Waive fees*

- *Implement process improvement teams to learn why mistakes happen and how to fix them*

- *Send something to a customer using Federal Express*

- *Offer a $5 bonus to a customer's account if the credit union has made a mistake or cannot fulfill a customer's request*

- *Put a customer on a team to help find a solution to make a process more effective*

The **University of Wisconsin Credit Union,** *Madison, Wisconsin, also lets employees waive fees. And, instead of blaming each other for mistakes, employees are encouraged to ask questions. Each work group conducts quality forums where employees can talk about ways to improve the quality of service.*
Says Donna Warner, Special Projects Coordinator, "Now, people are much more aware of how work is performed. They collect necessary data on their own. I've seen relationships improve. People have learned what responsibility is."

"cascading effect." The collection department doesn't realize it was the CU's fault. It sends out a late notice, creating extra work and most likely upsetting the member. Then another employee has to step in and locate the problem, find a solution, and calm down the member. By not working together, departments can create rework, dissatisfied members, and frustrated employees.

Instead, quality can be better achieved through teamwork. Interdepartmental communication and cooperation form an essential component of TQM. One way to do this is through cross-functional teams.

METHODS

In addition to understanding the philosophical side of quality, employees must be educated in the scientific approach to improving quality. Methods help managers and employees identify areas for improvement and form the means by which they make the improvements. Quality methods include quality circles, team meetings, and the Seven-Step Improvement Process.

The Seven-Step Improvement Process is a problem-solving technique. It's extremely important, because if all the steps are not followed, the improvements made to the process will probably not be permanent.

The following step-by-step description comes from "7 Step Improvement Process: Overview Document" by Joe

Innovative Training Techniques

*The **University of Wisconsin Credit Union**, Madison, Wisconsin, has made a big commitment to training. It actually closes all of its credit union offices, except two drive-up locations, Wednesday morning.*

From 8–9:30, all UW Credit Union employees attend training sessions, called "TeamTeach." There are four rotating training agendas. The first Wednesday of the month is a general staff meeting with every credit union employee. Management covers a variety of items like upcoming promotions, quality training, and employee of the month awards.

The second Wednesday is held by each department head as a general department meeting. Many departments spend the time reinforcing the quality training of the week before.

The specific department managers use the third and fourth Wednesdays at their discretion. Sometimes it's technical or service training. And sometimes it's cross-training. For example, the accounting department may want to conduct a training sessions for tellers.

"We want all departments to work together and teach together," said David Rosen, Training Coordinator. "These training sessions allow employees from different departments a chance to interact face-to-face. Our staff really enjoys them. As for our members? We feel that even though we take an hour from them, we pay it back with better service."

Haefner, Shelly Hornback, Thea Hefty and Andrea Hughes. We've summarized the key points here; you can find a more complete explanation in the document available from CUNA & Affiliates.

Step One: Determine Project Theme

Begin by identifying processes that need improvement. Look for ideas in customer inputs, worker/manager inputs, corporate strategic directives, or databases. Then determine the theme, which will have a direction, a process, and a measure. For example, a theme might be "to reduce the amount of time to complete a credit card application." The direction is "reduce," the process is "credit card application," and the measure is "time."

Step Two: Observe the Current Situation

First, examine the key features of the problem from several perspectives. To do this, study how the work is done now, develop theories that explain why the problem is happening, and collect and chart data to support these theories.

Step Three: Analyze the Root Causes

This step is the most important and the most time-consuming of all the steps. Here you develop the theories by diagramming the cause-and-effect relationships, and refining the diagram of causes. Then you prioritize the theories for root causes, collect and integrate information to verify the theories, and rewrite the problem based on the information you collected.

---

*At **Spokane Teachers Credit Union** in Spokane, Washington, training means more than time and money. It means fun.*

Spokane Teachers designed an innovative board game, called KABOOMBA!®, to teach product and service knowledge to employees. As an additional benefit, it also develops communication skills and encourages teamwork. Employees learn the value of providing members with accurate information about products and services and that it's okay to ask a co-worker for help. A typical question in KABOOMBA!® would be, "What is the minimum balance to open a checking account?" The accuracy of the answer determines whether a member (symbolized by a game piece) is saved at the credit union or lost to a competitor.

KABOOMBA!® has really become a part of the employee language at Spokane Teachers. Now, employees are more likely to ask for help when dealing with members rather than guessing or saying they don't know. KABOOMBA!® also won a Golden Mirror Award for Quality Service Improvement.

Though it might be time-consuming, it is extremely important to find the right root causes. If you don't, your improvements will be insignificant.

Step Four: Develop Improvements

Start by selecting the improvements you want to make. To do this, generate various alternative solutions, and pick one or more to further analyze. Next plan, schedule, and budget the improvements.

Step Five: Verify Results

Always begin by implementing the improvement on a small scale as a pilot program. That way, you can test your improvements to see if they really will make a difference. Study the results of the pilot program, and amend the improvements if necessary. Then implement it on a full scale. Again, verify the results of the full-scale approach.

Step Six: Standardize Improvements

This is a very important step in the process. If this step is skipped, chances are any improvements made will be lost over time. First, decide what you are going to measure—time, quantity, volume—then determine how you are going to measure the measurements.

Step Seven: Conclude the Project

Last, but not least, you need to conclude the process by checking the results, describing what was learned, and making plans for future improvement.

TOOLS

Tools are instruments used for solving problems. Peter Scholtes in the *Team Quality Handbook* says that quality tools "help your team visualize a process, pin-point problems, tend their causes and determine solutions. They also provide a way to evaluate proposed changes." Tools help both identify and analyze problems. Some examples of quality tools are time plots, flow charts, control charts, Pareto diagrams, brainstorming, multi-voting and Nominal Group Process.

Cross-functional Teams

Getting departments to talk to each other is always a challenge. **North Island Federal Credit Union,** *Chula Vista, California, tackles this problem by promoting department communication through cross-functional teams.*
A cross-functional team is composed of employees from finance, operations, marketing, and member service. Once a month they meet to discuss lending issues, new products or services, or process improvements. Departments now have a chance to talk to each other, and to have a say in other credit union concerns.
"This is an excellent quality tool," said Geri Dillingham, Senior Vice President of Marketing.
"Cross-functional teamwork is essential for the success of any quality program. At NIFCU, we find that projects run much more smoothly and productively when all areas affected by the change are represented. The relationships built during these types of team-building sessions are invaluable."

APPLICATIONS

The application is the actual attempt to improve a process. It is the implementation of a proposed change using knowledge of the principles, the system, the methods, the tools and the practice.

```
            Practice
          Tools
        Methods
      System
    Principles
```

Total Quality

Figure 2. **Pyramid Diagram**
© 1993 Mark P. Finster

Another Point Of View

Mark P. Finster *is a professor of business at the University of Wisconsin-Madison and a TQM consultant for businesses in the U.S. and abroad. He offers here comments on various aspects of TQM.*

Quality principles

"I don't think you can say you have a set of principles that are guiding you but not know them, or [not] have them written down, because then they can't possibly be guiding you. What usually happens is, companies say 'Yeah, we're principle-based.' And then if you ask seven different people what their principles are, you get seven different sets of principles. They're not guided by common principles, and of course that means they all have different themes, different values, and they're not going in the same direction."

Continuous improvement

"Quality is something that is on a continuum. And whatever level quality you have, you can raise that level of quality. And that's what continuous improvement says."

Member service

"I think as a movement, credit unions have been member-focused. But, there are many opportunities for them to improve what they're doing. And they're doing that, too. They are improving. Total quality has to do with how you're improving the rate of improvement."

CHOOSING A QUALITY CAMP

Credit union managers who seek to improve quality in their branch or throughout the institution will never find themselves at a loss for information. Immersing oneself in available literature will provide the platform for more intense and directed training and study. In fact, choosing a direction may be the most difficult part of starting a TQM initiative.

The wealth of information available today makes finding information easier, but may also serve to confuse as much as to help. One might question what quality managers did before they could contact the nearest consulting firm and order the garden variety TQM program. A decade ago, TQM did not occupy a separate aisle in national bookstore chains. In fact, many managers had not yet heard about the approach. Early TQM advocates had a voice, but managers had to go out of their way to hear it. Often, managers who subscribed to TQM training and education did not set out looking for the ultimate TQM program. Rather, they found it while they were searching for a way to apply quality in their organization.

Choosing a TQM Camp—One Credit Union's Story

Cherry Point Federal Credit Union, Havelock, North Carolina, formalized its TQM effort three years ago. Because Cherry Point serves a Marine Corps base, and the Marine Corps (as well as the Department of the Navy) was implementing W. Edwards Deming's philosophy, Cherry Point was able to share some of the expertise and training available on the base. So, it too, uses the Deming approach. Because the roots of Deming's 14 Points are grounded in manufacturing, the credit union has had some difficulty applying and adapting some of Deming's teachings. For instance: "Cease dependence on inspection to achieve quality." Credit unions don't produce widgets, they provide financial services. It's impossible to "cease inspection" when you must balance your books and audit your ledgers.

Cherry Point defines quality as "meeting or exceeding what a
(continued)

Undoubtedly, anyone researching quality twenty years ago happened upon the names W. Edwards Deming and Joseph M. Juran. In the early eighties, another thinker entered the mix—Philip B. Crosby. You will encounter these three TQM theorists in your research. They represent different perspectives on the components of TQM. You will notice some common threads in their theories and find areas where their theories differ. It is important to remember, however, that all three thinkers agree that TQM consists of principles, systems, methods, tools, and applications.

Once an organization chooses a TQM camp, its employees often become staunch supporters of that camp. They may even regard any other TQM approach as erroneous, and attack the tenets of other camps. Until you can evaluate each approach on its own merits, you may endure some confusion at the hands of enthusiastic advocates of a particular point of view. For instance, you might hear a Deming devotee say that Crosby's methods are fine for beginners but won't take an organization into maturity. Crosby supporters, on the other hand, might say that Deming's theories apply to the manufacturing industry more than the service industry and place too much emphasis on statistical methods of measuring results. Faced with these conflicts, some credit unions may decide to take the best of each approach and fashion a tailor-made TQM initiative.

reasonable member has the right to expect." So ultimately, only the member can define quality. So far, Cherry Point has had impressive results. It implemented eight different employee teams to study processes within the credit union. They recommended thirty-nine ways to improve processes; thirty-six of those have been approved for a 92.3% acceptance rate. This translates to employee empowerment and job satisfaction, in addition to improving quality service for members.

Wm. C. "Chris" Lindelof, President/ CEO, said, "On a scale of one to ten, I would rate us a nine in terms of our commitment and efforts to embrace quality. Certainly there are areas we are striving to improve, there are things we would do differently, but that's what the pursuit of quality is all about. There are no tens because quality is a journey, not a destination."

There are organizations and associations that exist to help credit unions find information on TQM. One organization in particular, GOAL/QPC in Massachusetts, researches and publishes information on using methods and tools within a TQM system. Because it focuses on the "best practices" of companies successful at TQM, its information is pragmatic, understandable, and free of the guru controversy. (See TQM Associations and Awards, at the back of this book.)

THE QUALITY GURUS

The following section introduces the main ideas of W. Edwards Deming, Joseph M. Juran and Philip B. Crosby.

W. EDWARDS DEMING

Definition of Quality

Deming does not offer a succinct definition of quality. Rather, he offers an explanation that quality is a value judgment made by a person who uses a product. He describes quality from the point of view of the employee and the point of view of the customer.

Quality to production workers means that their performance satisfies them and provides pride of workmanship.

Therefore, the maker of the product must consider the needs of the customer and turn those needs into measurable characteristics. Anyone endeavoring to produce a product must consider how that product will bring satisfaction at a price the user will pay (Deming, 1986).

Major Contributions

W. Edwards Deming came to the forefront of business management circles in the early 1980s when the NBC documentary, "If Japan Can Do It, Why Can't We?" focused on his management theories. During this program, America learned that Deming provided Japan with valuable consultation that proved paramount in maneuvering Japan's economic recovery after World War II. Viewers also saw that at least one U.S. company was making progress by putting Deming's tools into action. New Hampshire-based Nashua Corporation invited Deming to help with its quality efforts. During the program, viewers learned how Nashua Corporation President William Conway sought Deming's help to introduce a quality orientation into the company.

That single television program put Deming on the map in America, but his contributions started decades before this program aired.

Deming pioneered his approach to managing for quality back in the late 1920s.

A physicist turned statistician, Deming's early career started at the U.S. Department of Agriculture. There, some colleagues introduced him to Walter Shewhart, whose work focused on controlling quality by understanding variance. This introduction proved influential in Deming's later theories. Shewhart, a statistician at Bell Laboratories, had devised a formula for predicting the inherent standard fluctuations in product quality. According to Shewhart's model, anything outside the standard variation indicates an area for improvement. Production improves as variance of quality is reduced.

Deming began to study Shewhart's ideas and learn his techniques. He believed Shewhart's methods could best serve a company if all employees were educated to measure and chart variance in their daily work, thus giving them direct control over quality improvement. (Walton pp. 6, 7). Deming had his first opportunity to teach Shewhart's methods when he was invited by the U.S. government to propose a quality training program to help with wartime efforts during World War II. Soon, Deming was traveling around the country teaching Shewhart's methods to engineers and others involved in wartime production inspection.

Deming might have introduced quality to the western world back in the 1940s when he initially put forth many of his statistical methods, but his approach to quality management quickly lost ground in post-war America. Americans were too busy making money. At that time, competition wasn't a great concern, and managers did not see a need to break from the status quo.

The story might have ended there, but while America enjoyed a period of non-competition and turned to other styles of management, Deming's research and ideas helped pull Japan out of its economic crisis. News of his quality improvement methods had traveled across the Pacific, and Deming was invited by an association of prominent engineers, JUSE (Union of Japanese Science and Engineering), to help master a plan for Japan's economic recovery following the war. Deming immersed himself in the task and within five years, Japan was well on its way to economic recovery. For his efforts in the transformation, Deming received Japan's highest award, the Second Order Medal of the Sacred Treasure. Japan also established an award to recognize excellence in quality, it was named the Deming Prize.

Deming has authored numerous books and papers on quality. Now in his nineties, he continues to consult worldwide.

Overview

Deming believes achieving quality is a process of continuous improvement. The quality of a product or service is improved by controlling variance of outcome. He identifies two kinds of variance: chance and special. Chance is defined as the defects or variations in products and services over which we have no control. He believes companies waste time if they look for chance variation.

Instead, Deming advocates concentrating on finding special variation—the problems that have assignable causes and variation. He teaches managers and employees how to identify assignable variation and create a work environment where all employees can take responsibility for identifying problems and solutions, thereby achieving process improvement.

Deming's 14 Principles For Transformation

Most TQM advocates agree that a quality transformation depends on management's commitment and vision. But a simple commitment is not enough. Deming believes that managers need to know more to what they are committing. Simply saying they believe in quality or putting quality first will not make it happen. Deming abhors motivational slogans and exhortations because they usually amount to motivational quick-fix solutions and do not translate into long-term results.

Deming has devised a list of fourteen basic points or principles about quality that he believes managers must adopt for a successful transformation. These principles are at the heart of his teaching. They apply to all types of organizations, including small and large, manufacturing and service, and to all levels of management. Deming expounds on these "14 Points" in his writings, but we've adapted them here for your reference. (You can find a full description of them in his book, *Out of the Crisis,* pp. 23, 24.) They include:

1. **Create constancy of purpose toward improvement of product and service.**

   It's easy for management to become caught up with the day-to-day details of business. Focusing on the future will keep the company alive over the long run. Credit unions must innovate, overcome regulatory and competitive obstacles, put resources into research and education, and constantly improve on services and products that will ensure their place in the future.

2. **Adopt the new philosophy.**

   Credit unions must accept the challenges of a new economic age. In order to succeed, none of us can continue to tolerate the inadequacies of American management. We must accept and embrace change.

3. **Cease dependence on mass inspection.**

   Inspection does not improve quality; it identifies mistakes and areas for rework. Quality processes should be employed before the inspection stage.

4. **End the practice of awarding business on the basis of price tag alone.**

   The factors of quality and service should be considered with every purchase. A contract awarded to the lowest bidder may not be the best value. American businesses must explore the opportunities of a long-term supplier relationship.

5. Improve constantly and forever the system of production and service.

Quality starts at the design stage, before a product or service is delivered to the market. Every product, service, and method should be regarded as one of a kind.

6. Institute training on the job.

Management needs to understand every aspect of the business to enable workers to carry out their jobs with satisfaction. Management must provide the kind of leadership and training that lets employees know what their jobs consist of.

7. Adopt and institute leadership.

The job of management is not supervision, but leadership. Management must work on sources of improvement, the intent of quality of product and service, and on the translation of the intent into design and the actual product. Deming argues that management is responsible for 85% of the problems in business.

8. Drive out fear.

Employees will not develop their best performance until they feel secure and free to express ideas and ask questions without reprisals.

9. Break down barriers between staff areas.

Teamwork is sorely needed throughout the company. Teamwork requires that employees compensate for each other's strengths and weaknesses.

10. Eliminate slogans, exhortations, and targets for the work force.

Deming believes that exhortations and posters like "Do it right the first time" generate frustration and resentment. They advertise to the production worker that management is unaware of the barriers to pride of workmanship. As the workers see it, management expects workers to perform what managers themselves are unable to do. Instead of using slogans, Deming suggests that management demonstrate a way to provide workers with the tools they need to perform the job.

11a. Eliminate numerical quotas for the work force.
11b. Eliminate numerical quotas for people in management.

A quota is a fortress against improvement of quality and productivity. Quotas do not help people do a better job. They do not address quality of workmanship or provide suggestions for improvement.

12. Remove barriers that rob people of pride of workmanship.

People have become a commodity. Management may hire an employee

at a posted price, or may not,
depending on the need. If employees
are not needed, they go back on the
market. We must move beyond this
mentality. Managers must be ready
to help workers overcome the
barriers to doing their jobs. Managers need to listen to employees'
input. When employees feel important to a job, they will make every
effort to be successful on the job.
Employees will feel important to a
job if they can take pride in their
work and have a part in improving
the system. Absenteeism and
turnover of the work force are
largely the result of poor supervision and poor management.

13. Encourage education and self-improvement for everyone.

What an organization needs is not
just good people; it needs people
who are improving with education.
More than simply requiring money,
people require everbroadening
opportunities to add something to
society, both materially and
otherwise.

14. Take action to accomplish the transformation.

Do it. Put the principle to work
every day. Take action to complete
the transformation.

Educating your Employees

State Employees Credit Union in *Raleigh, North Carolina, demonstrates its commitment to training its employees through education. Employees are encouraged to educate themselves either by getting a college degree, a CCUE designation, or pursuing other fields of study not directly related to their job.*

All employees are required to complete a basic module on credit union techniques. After that, they can complete other advanced modules, which are not related to their job. For each module they complete, they receive a bonus.

Employees then have the opportunity to become a Certified Credit Union Executive. State Employees CU pays for everything except for books. When they receive their CCUE designation, their annual salary is increased.

After they get their CCUE designation, they can attend college to get a bachelor's or a master's degree. Again, State Employee pays for any business-related courses. After graduation, employees again receive a raise in salary.

Mark Twisdale, Senior Vice-President of Staff Development, said "we don't require employees to increase their education, we simply provide them with the opportunity to do something to better themselves and make them a more valuable employee."

Take Action

The last of the 14 Points bears additional mention because it includes what Deming calls "a plan for action." It is the means by which quality improvement takes place. (According to Deming, quality improvement never ends, and it doesn't happen overnight.) Deming proposes several steps for taking action.

First, management must understand how the 14 Points apply to their business. They must make a conscious effort to come to a common understanding of them, agree to adopt them, and adhere to them. They must break with the old ways and habits that prevent the company from moving ahead. Management also must understand and watch for the seven deadly diseases and obstacles.

Deadly Diseases And Obstacles

Dr. Deming has been known to refuse to consult with an organization that he believes lacks the seriousness to forge ahead with a quality transformation. That's because without commitment to follow his 14 Points, Deming believes a transformation effort is doomed for failure. In fact, Deming identifies seven obstacles to achieving quality; he believes American management suffers from these "deadly diseases." A quality effort is bound to fail, unless it "cures" these diseases:

- Lack of constancy of purpose

- Emphasis on short-term profits

- Evaluation of performance, merit rating, or annual review

- Mobility of top management

- Running a company on visible figures alone

- Excessive medical costs

- Excessive costs of warranty, fueled by lawyers that work on contingency fees

Chain Reaction

Deming suggests that quality starts a chain reaction of events that ultimately leads to an increase in employment. The chain reaction begins when management agrees to adopt Deming's 14 Points. As management improves quality, costs go down. As a result, productivity improves. Thus, the company is able to meet the market with better quality products and services and lower prices. A more competitive position enables the company to stay in business and therefore produce more jobs (Walton 23–25).

System of Profound Knowledge

Knowledge forms the basis for Deming's transformation model. Management must seek knowledge, use it, and share it. Expecting everyone to work hard and do their best does not always work.

Deming suggests that management and employees must understand what he calls the "System of Profound Knowledge." It consists of four parts:

- Appreciation for a system

- Knowledge of variation

- Theory of knowledge

- Knowledge of psychology

Each part of the system of Profound Knowledge builds on the other. When combined, the four areas form the foundation for the quality transformation.

Deming describes *appreciation for a system* as the electrical system of a car. Each activity or system depends on the others to run properly. Systems of either a car or a business cannot exist in a vacuum. He explains *knowledge of variation* as an understanding of the common causes and assignable causes of variation. Variation exists everywhere; in other words, no two snowflakes are alike. Employees should know how to identify variation and when to take action to improve a process. Deming maintains that employees should be instructed to identify assignable variation and to improve it with tools. Learning to use these tools requires the third part of the system of Profound Knowledge, *theory of knowledge*. Deming's theory of knowledge recognizes that virtually every move we make is based on a prediction of a certain outcome, and, occasionally, the predicted outcome does not occur. Deming proposes that we can learn something about a process by comparing results to the predicted outcome. He calls this the P–D–C–A (Plan–Do–Check–Act) cycle. Deming offers the fourth part of the system of Profound Knowledge to promote teamwork. *Knowledge of psychology* recognizes that all people are different and therefore, we learn and become motivated in different ways.

Strengths

Deming provides a strong philosophy to bolster his system for quality management improvement. He can provide specific examples of successful applications of his system. We know what he did for Japan.

Weaknesses

Some critics say that Deming's philosophy works better for manufacturing companies fashioned after processes that are closely linked to numerical data. Companies in the service industry have a harder time quantifying their results.

Some managers say Deming's approach is too statistical, that it's not human enough and does not offer step-by-step ways to approach the transformation.

Response to Critics

Deming claims that his philosophy does work for service organizations. He devotes an entire chapter to quality and productivity in service organizations in his book, *Out of the Crisis*. He also points out that census figures indicate approximately 75 out of 100 people are employed by service industries. He also notes that among the winners of the Deming Prize are several service organizations.

J. M. JURAN

Definition of Quality

Juran notes numerous definitions of quality, and recognizes the following two definitions as the most important for managers to understand:

Product features—The better the product features are, the better the quality.

Freedom from deficiencies—The fewer the deficiencies, the better the quality.

He offers the phrase "fitness for use" as a shorthand for the longer definitions.

Major Contributions

Juran is a contemporary of Deming's; the two men were influenced by many of the same people and events during their early careers. Juran was born in 1904, studied electrical engineering and law, and embarked on a career at Western Electric's Hawthorne Plant. During his first two years with Western Electric, Juran was part of a team that investigated complaints within the plant and in the field.

Juran's interest in quality heightened when he was one of a group of approximately twenty Western Electric engineers educated in the use of statistical measures to control the quality of manufactured goods. He learned to use and apply the Shewhart Control Chart, a statistical tool used to measure variance of quality. According to Walter Shewhart, who de-

vised this measurement tool, every product will produce a predictable, standard variance in quality. Problems in quality appear as excess outside the norm. The Shewhart chart provided a way to track fluctuations outside the norm and study them to find out why a product lacked quality.

During World War II, Juran worked for the federal government as an assistant lend-lease administrator and an assistant foreign economic administrator. During this time he observed two positive influences on quality: the uses of sampling inspection tables and extensive training to introduce workers to statistical quality control. He also observed what happened when management went overboard with statistical control by using the method without understanding how to apply the results, or when management neglected to educate the work force and gain overall acceptance. Juran believes early attempts to use statistical control as a means of quality improvement failed because the efforts became isolated in a quality control group. Management did not properly educate the entire work force, and therefore many people rejected the methods or used them improperly.

These experiences and observations helped Juran form his theories of quality management and stress the importance of establishing teams to solve problems and make improvements. He left the government service after about five years and began free-lancing as a quality consultant. He became widely known in management groups and associations.

As did Deming, Juran played a significant role in Japan's economic recovery. In 1981, Japan awarded him the Order of the Sacred Treasure. In 1992, the president of the United States awarded Juran the National Medal of Technology. He continues to consult and write and has received numerous other medals to commemorate his achievements. He is founder and chairman of the Juran Institute.

Overview

Juran believes that companies must chart a course for managing quality by realizing a system that permeates all levels of management, departments, and product lines. He suggests managing quality on a project-by-project basis.

Juran Trilogy

Juran focuses on three basic quality-oriented processes which he believes are universal in business, and which cut across all functions, levels, and product lines: Quality Planning, Quality Control, and Quality Improvement. Juran says each of the processes in the trilogy is vital to improvement and all are carried out by an unwavering set of activities. He believes that understanding how each step in the trilogy interrelates, and then balancing the importance of the steps will naturally lead to quality. Juran advocates applying the steps to training and strategic business planning. The basic steps in the quality processes follow (Juran, *Quality Progress,* August 1986, p. 21); they include:

Quality Planning

The planning process can be applied to any aspect (process) of business:

1. Identify the customers, both internal and external

2. Determine customer needs

3. Develop product features that respond to customer needs

4. Establish quality goals that meet the needs of customers and suppliers alike, and do so at the minimum combined cost

5. Develop a process that can produce the needed product features

6. Prove process capability—prove that the process can meet the quality goals under normal operating conditions

Quality Control

Juran defines quality control as running the process at optimal effectiveness:

- Choose control subjects—what to control

- Choose units of measurement

- Establish measurement

- Establish standards of performance

- Measure actual performance

- Interpret the difference

- Take action on the difference

Quality Improvement/Breakthrough

Juran talks about quality improvement and breakthrough as interdependent parts of a process. He defines quality improvement as the organized creation of beneficial change, and breakthrough as improvement of performance to an unprecedented level.

An improvement happens on a project-by-project basis. An improvement is considered a breakthrough if it surpasses previous standard levels of performance (Juran, Gryna, Bingham, 1951). Juran identifies two criteria for a breakthrough: the new level of performance must be new (never attained before), and the improvement is the result of human determination, not luck.

Juran's series of universal steps for achieving quality improvement/breakthrough performance (Juran, 1986, 1992) are offered here:

- Establish policies and environment for improvement

- Identify specific projects for improvement

- Organize teams to guide the projects

- Diagnose to find the causes

- Provide remedies

- Prove that the remedies are effective under operating conditions

- Establish controls to hold the gains

Spiral of Progress

All products and services are generated by a spiral of events, a progression of activities that build upon one another. These activities involve people at every level of the company as the product moves from conception to completion. Since quality is derived from cooperation and interrelation throughout all levels of the spiral, it is important that people involved in the process at each turn of the spiral know the specifications for their contribution.

Pareto Principle
(Vital Few, Trivial Many)

Juran refers to the Pareto Principle (or "the vital few and the trivial many") to describe the notion that problems or defects in business arise from a relatively small number of causes or factors. The theory originated from Vilfredo Pareto's mathematical formula for studying the unequal distribution of wealth. Juran applied Pareto's formula in a universal sense to study the general principle of unequal distribution in business. The theory illustrates that unequal distribution also applies to employee absenteeism, safety problems, and product defects, thus allowing the opportunity to study the few causes responsible for the majority of the problems (*Quality Progress,* May 1975, pp. 8–9).

Strengths

Juran provides clear roles and expectations for everyone involved in the transformation, from upper-level management through the front-line worker.

Weaknesses

His emphasis on establishing company-wide goals may leave too much open to interpretation and encourage management to set far-fetched objectives.

Response To Critics

A company must have a plan and know where it's headed. It must have a goal to strive toward.

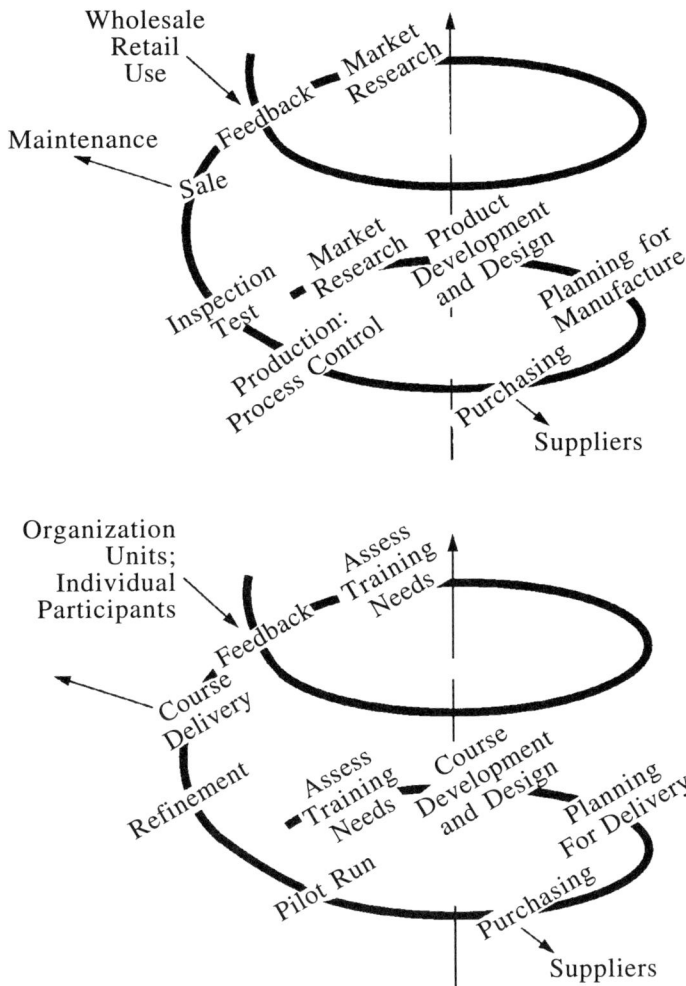

Figure 3. **Spiral Diagram**

Reproduced with permission from the copyright holder, Juran Institute, Inc., Wilton, Connecticut, 06897 USA.

P.B. CROSBY

Definition of Quality

Crosby defines quality as conformance to requirements. When requirements are clearly stated we can know if they are met. When quality is defined as conformance to requirements, quality problems become nonconformance problems and quality becomes definable. (Crosby, *Quality Is Free,* 1980, p. 15).

Major Contributions

Crosby's quality career spans a forty-year period, beginning with his service in the Navy during World War II and the Korean War. He later moved to the private sector and served in a number of positions, moving from the assembly line to quality manager of Martin Marietta. Working in this capacity for eight years, he created his concept of "zero defects."

Then Crosby took a job as a manager at ITT, where he was charged with the task of implementing a company-wide quality program. He developed his quality concepts and applied them at more than 500 companies worldwide. He determined that the focus of quality improvement programs should include: quality control, reliability, quality engineering, supplier quality, inspection, product qualification, training, testing, consumer affairs, ability improvement, and metrology. He calls this the "integrity systems table." It "rests" on four legs: management participation and attitude, professional quality management, original problems, and recognition.

Crosby has authored eight books, including the best-seller, *Quality Is Free.* In 1979, he founded Philip Crosby Associates (PCA), Inc., one of the largest consulting firms in the world. Now retired, Crosby writes and speaks on quality, and has established a new venture, Career IV, Inc.

Overview

Prevention is the key to quality.

Zero Defects/Do It Right the First Time

The main thrust of Crosby's approach to quality emphasizes managing to prevent defects. His theme, "Do it right the first time," is a goal that sets a performance standard for managing quality. Crosby explains that zero defects is not an exhortation, but an expectation. He says managers and workers have come to expect error and spend too much time and money managing the errors instead of preventing them. Instead, they should aim for a standard of zero defects. He does not advocate that leadership adopt an acceptable quality level for products and services because this implies that error is expected. Rather, he stresses the importance of managers educating employees and encouraging them to adopt the zero defects attitude.

Quality Is Free

"Quality is free. It's not a gift, but it is free. What costs money are the unquality things—all the actions that involve not doing the job right the first time," (Crosby, 1979).

Crosby evaluates the cost of quality in terms of the expense of nonconformance to standards. He says quality makes profit because money that doesn't go into fixing a problem gets added to the bottom line.

Absolutes of Quality Management

Crosby sets forth his own basic tenets of quality (Crosby, 1980, p. 111) as follows:

- Quality means conformance, not elegance

- There is no such thing as a quality problem

- There is no such thing as the economics of quality; it is always cheaper to do the job right the first time

- The only performance measurement is the cost of quality

- The only performance standard is zero defects

Fourteen Steps to Quality Improvement

Crosby does not believe a company will achieve zero defects overnight. He says quality improvement takes time and effort, and it takes a commitment from management to keep everyone focused. He advocates a fourteen-step plan to achieving quality (Crosby, 1988, pp. 112–119).

Is Quality Culturally Defined?— Japanese vs. American Quality

Is quality different in America than it is in Japan? We know both countries continually strive to improve the quality of their products. But do cultural influences motivate each differently? And can we improve quality by understanding the cultural influences on our perception of quality?

Several quality experts and theorists have wrestled with questions such as these, and offer some useful information about achieving quality in America.

Quality experts Lewis Hatala and Marilyn Zuckerman set out to uncover what they believed was the heart of quality in America. The authors were employed at AT&T during its divestiture in the mid-eighties, when the company faced tough competition and made the transition from copper-cable to fiber-optic technology. In their book, Incredibly American, *the authors relate their attempts to understand the meaning of quality in America and ultimately, to make total quality a corporate reality at AT&T.*

Hatala and Zuckerman studied success stories to uncover the common elements that led to winning results. They looked for patterns in the stories to see if they could reproduce the elements of success. The quality experts discovered the American "archetype" or culturally defined predisposition toward the concept of quality. Americans like a challenge, and we always root for the

(continued)

1. Management Commitment

Initially, managers must become aware of the need for a quality improvement program. Once they've agreed to the commitment, they should draw up a quality policy that is communicated and adopted by everyone in the company.

2. Quality Improvement Team

Appoint a quality improvement leader for each department and educate them.

3. Quality Measurement

Use statistical or other quantitative measurement to record the status of quality in every department and show areas for improvement.

4. Cost of Quality Evaluation

Determine the expense of doing things wrong—establish a basis for improvement.

5. Quality Awareness

Communicate to employees the cost of nonconformance.

6. Corrective Action

Establish meetings where employees can discuss problems and offer solutions.

underdog. We work hard, but lose our enthusiasm when the problem is nearly solved. We need a constant challenge in order to maintain our interest in achieving our final goal. We often fall short of producing quality because as a project approaches completion, we no longer experience the challenge. We lack motivation to produce excellence.

In Japan, however, people are motivated by different cultural influences. The satisfaction of shaping a product to perfection is motivation enough. Hatala and Zuckerman found that to Americans, quality means "it works." In Japan, on the other hand, quality means "perfection." Americans need an extra push to reach the point of perfection in terms of product quality.

These observations are born out in the work of Japanese quality control expert and academician Kaoru Ishikawa. He observed that in the sixties, when the U.S. Department of Defense tried to establish a "zero defects" (ZD) standard for American supply companies, the effort failed, largely because the standard was forced upon suppliers and not adopted by the work force (Ishikawa, 1985). The government tried to force suppliers to adopt zero defects without educating them about the quality process. Among a list of numerous reasons for failure, Ishikawa includes, "The word 'kickoff' in the zero defects movement sounded fine. But wasn't it another term for commanding and forcing the workers to start a

(continued)

7. Establish an Ad Hoc Committee for the Zero Defects Program

Appoint a committee to develop a plan for communicating zero defects to the company.

8. Supervisor Training

Educate all managers about the steps to achieve quality.

9. Zero Defects Day

Communicate zero defects throughout the company on the same day.

10. Goal Setting

With their supervisors, each employee will develop goals and guidelines for achievement.

11. Error Cause Removal

Individuals record problems that prevent them from achieving error-free work.

12. Recognition

Establish an awards program to recognize employees who meet their performance goals or perform an extraordinary act.

13. Quality Councils

Quality consultants and team leaders meet regularly to assess progress and chart new ways to improve programs.

campaign for which they had very little enthusiasm?"
Hatala and Zuckerman concluded in their study that Americans can motivate themselves to higher levels of performance, and thus achieve quality, by identifying and striving for nearly impossible goals. As one goal nears completion, Americans must redefine the parameters so the next goal can once again seem beyond reach. The constant drive for success will move us toward perfection.

14. Do It Over Again

The fourteen steps will be completed within a year to eighteen months. Once a company has completed all the steps, it's time to start the program anew by holding a zero defects anniversary, reeducating employees and management, and appointing new representatives.

Quality Management Maturity Grid

Crosby designed a system for evaluating the progress of a quality initiative (Crosby, 1992). The system follows a grid format and allows someone to evaluate the maturity level of a company's quality initiative at a glance. Crosby suggests that managers use the grid to convince upper management of the need for a formalized TQM program, and to help companies evaluate their progress toward quality improvement. The grid rates the company's maturity in six different categories: management understanding and attitude, quality organization status, problem handling, cost of quality as a percent of sales, quality improvement actions, and summation of company quality posture. These stages of maturity progress from stage I, uncertainty; stage II, awakening; stage III, enlightenment; stage IV, wisdom; to stage V, certainty.

Strengths

Some managers like Crosby's approach because it's easy to follow. His fourteen steps offer a "cookbook approach" to TQM.

His approach is easy to sell to upper management because it shows how TQM affects the bottom line.

Weaknesses

Critics say that adhering to a zero defects philosophy won't necessarily ensure a quality product. A product may meet specifications and be free of defects, but it still may not contain any value to the customer.

Others say zero defects is nothing but a slogan full of hype that cannot sustain a long-term commitment to quality.

Response to Critics

Crosby adamantly states that zero defects is not a motivational program (Crosby, 1979). It is a means of communicating that everyone should strive to do things right the first time. He also states that a quality improvement effort must be well planned, and implemented over a long period of time. He acknowledges that a quality transformation requires a culture change.

TQM IN THE CREDIT UNION–WHY NOW?

Several factors make TQM an important choice for credit unions now; they include the recession, new technology, higher expectations, increased opportunity, and competition. The deregulation in the early eighties opened up new challenges for the nineties. Credit unions now offer a full range of saving, lending, and related services that provide members with a host of new opportunities. And the scope of credit union activity continues to expand.

But deregulation was a double-edged sword. Greater opportunity also demands greater responsibility. Credit unions are learning to contend with numerous decisions—dividend and interest rates, investments and liquidity needs, service offerings, and a host of operational matters. Loan-to-share ratios are down, and fewer borrowers mean more competition.

Deregulation also opened the door for new competition with other financial institutions. To the consumer, the line between credit unions and competitors was blurred. Now, more than ever, credit unions need to make ourselves distinct from the competition by staying true to our members and our purpose. We need

---

Innovative Processes for Member Service

Members are the reason for a credit union's existence. Meeting members' needs with innovative solutions helps attract new members and retain old ones.

By streamlining processes, North Island Federal Credit Union, Chula Vista, California, has found a better way to serve its members. North Island met with suppliers, and branch and department employees to flowchart the process. And they found a faster way to approve loans. It reduced the loan approval process at a credit union lot car sale from three hours to forty-five minutes for members without pre-approval. Subsequent credit union car sales have been resoundingly successful.

One good way of finding out what's wrong with processes is to ask the people who use them—the employees. That's what John Deere Community Credit Union in Waterloo, Iowa, did. Employees suggested ways to improve processes via survey cards. Next, John Deere set up teams to

(continued)

to pay attention to bringing economic benefits to our members, giving members control, providing service at cost, and exercising social responsibility.

At the same time, we must realize that the competition is not relegated simply to the "us versus them" scenario encountered with the banking industry in the past. Credit unions now find themselves competing for membership and assets. We're in the midst of a shake-up, where weaker credit unions will be forced to improve, merge, or liquidate. The stronger credit unions will see their memberships rise, while the total number of credit unions will drop.

During this time of change, credit unions can turn to TQM as a means of survival, to expand and strengthen their memberships, control costs, find the competitive edge to anticipate changes in the marketplace, and provide members with innovative services and solutions for their financial needs.

All credit unions share common activities. Eventually, through TQM, credit unions will develop systems to optimize their performance. These systems might include teller training, or fulfilling member requests. They might also include solutions to common critical work processes, tools for measuring whether or not the processes are meeting members' needs, and methods for responding to common problems that might occur.

If TQM is introduced effectively, the credit union will be incredibly dynamic, with the motivation, morale, enthusiasm, and ability to continue to improve and to satisfy members' needs.

---

examine the processes that the employees had flagged. One process it improved involved members whose partners recently died. Before, the members had to close their account and open a new one. This added stress to the already grieving member, as well as created rework for everyone. Now, an employee can simply change the name on the account.

Focusing on Your Members

*Focusing on meeting and exceeding members' expectations is the heart of quality. Rex Johnson, of **Baxter Credit Union** in Deerfield, Illinois, shares some of the techniques his credit union uses.*

Lunch with the President

Once every two months, Baxter Credit Union springs for lunch. Rex and members of his management team travel all around the U.S. and Puerto Rico—wherever members and potential members are. The lunch is designed expressly to meet and listen to expectations. Baxter invites a group with only one caveat; guests must gather information from twenty of their peers about how Baxter CU is performing. Rex wants to know what the credit union is doing right, as well as what it is doing wrong. A member of the Baxter CU team takes notes on everything the members say, good and bad. The team brings the information home and circulates it to the entire staff. "This is an excellent way to find out what members really want," said Rex.   *(continued)*

Member Opportunity Form

Every time a member has a complaint, a Baxter Credit Union employee works with him or her to resolve the complaint. Then the employee completes a Member Opportunity Form that explains the situation and why the member was displeased. "The rationale behind designing a Member Opportunity Form was simply we don't know how good we can become until we know how bad we are," said Rex. Each day, these forms land on Rex's desk for review. This way he can stay in touch with Baxter CU's members. He reviews the forms and either personally calls the member or delegates it to the vice-president of quality. When necessary, an ad hoc team is assembled to review the process that caused the nonconformance and to build in prevention, not just corrective action. The department involved is always a part of the ad hoc team. This way, it becomes part of the solution.

The "Lunch Bunch"

A group of Baxter CU employees gather at lunch to call each and every member that closes an account. They want to know why the member closed the account and if there was something that the credit union could have done better. Usually, members close accounts because they misunderstand the credit union's rules. For example, they're leaving Baxter Corporation so they think they can't be a member of Baxter CU. So they just close their accounts. The Lunch Bunch phone call affords the opportunity to better understand the rules. Most often, they are still eligible to be a member at Baxter CU. "This technique has been hugely successful at persuading members to come back. And we learn a lot about how we are doing, which has helped us change a number or process," Rex said.

GETTING STARTED

STUDY

Read books, magazine articles, and case studies. We've included a list of recommended books at the end of this primer. Borrow audio and video tapes from the library. Join an association committed to advancing the understanding of TQM. Talk to other CU managers who use quality concepts. Attend workshops. Choose the best method for your credit union.

START SLOWLY

As one credit union president explained, "You can walk circles around the pool, but eventually, you have to jump in the water." Communicate with employees early and often. They will have many questions and doubts. They may resist the change—especially at times when progress seems slow. "Don't we have enough to do? Why change? It just makes our lives more complicated." You may hear these comments; make sure you communicate your commitment to help. TQM is not a "program of the month"—it is a cultural transformation.

TQM Naysayers

*When the highly regarded corporate consulting firm **Arthur D. Little, Inc.** released data suggesting TQM doesn't always work, executives took notice. The firm based its report on a commissioned survey of 500 executives from manufacturing and service companies. The survey indicated that 93% of the executives polled had some form of quality improvement program. However, only one-third of those same executives said their company's TQM initiative had improved its competitive position.*

Does this mean TQM is on its way out? Is it a failure? Arthur D. Little, Inc. asked these same questions. It found that the failed initiatives were often halfhearted approaches.

As more companies join the fold of TQM converts, you'll come across more survey results, reporting both success and horror stories about TQM applications. In time, you'll learn how to evaluate these stories, know which to believe, and be able to identify valuable lessons to apply to your credit union.

(continued)

INTEGRATE

Quality is not a separate entity. It does not belong in a separate department. It is not a mission or program. Don't give it its own logo. It is a permanent mind-set that will permeate every area of your credit union.

SECURE BOARD OF DIRECTORS AND MANAGEMENT BUY-IN

Middle managers will probably be the most resistant. Our traditional school of management does not promote leadership that empowers, in fact, it often promotes using power instead of giving it. Train your management in the new school. For credit unions, this means also educating the members of the board. Let them know that they play a critical role in the success of the quality effort, and make sure they understand it by providing them with adequate education.

EDUCATE

Every consultant believes in an abundance of training. In this case, it is the foundation for making sure the TQM initiative stays on track.

EXERCISE PATIENCE

Quality provides one guarantee. It won't materialize overnight. Most experts

Critical surveys, reports, and articles can be helpful. Obviously, TQM isn't the only way to manage a business. It is simply an approach that works when a group of determined people follow all the guidelines. But like any endeavor, it is subject to failure. Listen to the critics. Read the studies. They might have something to say.

But be aware that the results are only as good as the source. Make sure you assess the critics as closely as they assess TQM. Is the critic reputable? Does the critic stand to gain by turning managers away from TQM? Some management consultants are losing business because they don't teach TQM, and they would gladly turn managers away from practicing it altogether.

For instance, there have been cases in which the Arthur D. Little survey has been taken out of context, and has become the basis of several widely distributed articles by consultants whose businesses have suffered because they did not adopt TQM. Some consultants reference only the parts of the survey that bolster their argument against TQM. They don't offer their readers the benefit of material that supports TQM as well.

One article that offered the Arthur D. Little survey as proof that TQM doesn't work neglected to tell readers that in Arthur D. Little's press release announcing the findings, another survey was cited that suggested companies failed due to their own mistakes.

(continued)

If readers had the benefit of analyzing the press release themselves, they would have learned that, in a survey of executives at leading medical companies, Arthur D. Little found that the companies cited numerous barriers to making further headway in their TQM initiatives. Among the most frequently cited obstacles were lack of commitment and cooperation from chief executive officers and other senior managers. Other barriers included unrealistic expectations, failure to focus on the needs of the external customers, failure to set priorities, a dearth of effective management tools, and failure to tie a firm's quality improvement into a long-term corporate strategy.

You'll also find all these obstacles listed in W. Edwards Deming's list of what he terms the "deadly diseases"—the obstacles to achieving total quality.

"The long and short of it," said an Arthur D. Little Vice-President in the press release, "is that the leadership and vision to inspire action must come from the chief executive in deeds as well as words." He noted that a transforming company will find the process of transformation invigorating, and that a transformed company can overtake the competition.

Read between the lines as often as possible. That way, you'll get closer to the complete story.

Another TQM Success Story

*In an economically dismal year, **AT&T Employees Federal Credit Union,** Bedminster, New Jersey, increased its loans by 30%. How did AT&T EFCU do it? Through hard work, targeting key strategies, and TQM.*

Process

AT&T EFCU realized it could improve its loan processes through reorganization. It centralized loan operations into a Headquarters Loan Center Unit and streamlined the process. All loans are handled there, not in the branches. Now, better loans with lower delinquency ratios are processed faster (approval in less than a hour) with fewer people.

Incentives

In 1990, AT&T EFCU began an employee incentive plan. The plan rewards both teams and individuals, and includes all employees.

Each incentive is designed to achieve a specific goal. For example, one goal was to review 97% of all consumer loans within 24 hours, and 99% of all auto loans within one hour. Those targets were met and each employee received a $100 bonus.

"Our incentive plan has generated tremendous results. Supported by on-going training on cross-selling skills as well as loan products, features, and benefits, our staff is motivated and confident in keeping our members better informed about our products. And they are focused on cross-selling our products and services," said Paul Fiore, Vice-President/CFO.

agree that it takes ten years to fully integrate quality and see significant results. Change is hard. You'll stumble. You'll get discouraged. Some managers will only pay lip service. Others may be worried that it will cost in the short term. Don't give up! People sometimes become impatient when they don't see change happening quickly or when they are not pleased with the initial results. They blame TQM, rather than evaluating their own success at implementing it.

QUALITY IS HERE TO STAY

Members are becoming more familiar with TQM. They expect it. If their own employers utilize it, they will certainly be looking for it. Here are some quality practices you will learn more about as your credit union begins its quality transformation.

WRITING A VISION STATEMENT

All credit unions need a vision of what they want to become. You cannot implement TQM today if you don't know where you are going to be tomorrow.

A good way to start writing your vision statement is to answer the question, "Where do we want our credit union to be in the future?" Take that answer and hone it until it becomes your vision statement.

STRATEGIC PLANNING

Strategic planning, or *hoshin* planning, makes quality management into total quality management. It puts into place your credit union's long- and medium-term goals. Upper-level managers begin by targeting Key Strategic Objectives (KSO) which sustain the organization's long-term direction. These KSOs travel down the organization to the workers, who decide the best strategy on fulfilling the KSOs. Those strategies travel back up the organization so the managers can give their approval. This way, everyone is given an opportunity to add their input on the company's long-term direction and how best to support that direction.

THE "PLAN–DO–CHECK–ACT CYCLE"

The whole purpose of the Plan–Do–Check–Act (PDCA) cycle is to illustrate quality's continuous improvement. Also known as the Deming cycle or the Shewhart cycle, the PDCA cycle can help us continually improve our products and services; each word is a step in the process.

Plan: Decide what process changes you are planning to make.

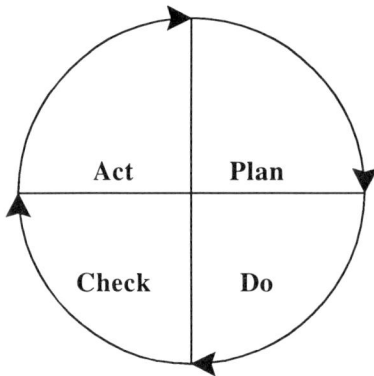

Figure 4. **PDCA Cycle***

Do: Test your change on a pilot audience. Make the audience as small as possible in case the change does not work.

Check: Collect and study data to see how effective (or ineffective) your change was.

Act: Examine your data to see how successful your changes were. Decide if you are going to keep your changes, throw them out, or go through the PDCA cycle again.

The PDCA cycle is very effective when used in its entirety. Unfortunately, many people (especially Americans) only use plan–do or do–act. Most of the time, Americans don't check their activities. Consequently, plan–do can make systems progressively worse or overly complicated. The problems continue because they're never examined. If you can avoid the temptation to skip the checking stage, you'll be more successful at changing your processes.

Quality "Work Smarter, Not Harder"

"If we don't understand the process, we'll end up with short-lived gains," said Joe Haefner, **CUNA Service Group.**

He relates a story about a company whose customers were complaining that they couldn't get through on the phone lines. So, the company decided to improve the process. It installed an automatic call distributing system (ACD) to find out the abandonment rate, or the percent of customers who hang up before getting answered. The ACD showed a very high and inconsistent abandonment rate. Management decided it had to be lowered to 4% by the end of one month. However, management changed nothing in the system to lower the rate. The goal became the driving force for the organization. Management encouraged employees to work harder to reach the goal. And the employees did. They answered phones faster, kept the length of the phone calls to a minimum, and put off some of their other work to concentrate on answering the phones. For one month, they lowered the rate to below 4%. Management threw the department a pizza party.
Management was preparing to set a lower goal. But the next day, the abandonment rate soared to above 8%.
What happened?
The group had worked harder, not smarter.

(continued)

---

* From W. Edward Deming's OUT OF THE CRISIS, 1986, MIT Press.

VIEWING WORK AS A PROCESS

In order to understand the work process you need to understand all the steps involved in the process (how the work flows), and know that the goal is to meet or exceed your customers' expectations. Everyone in a credit union has customers, whether they be external (your members) or internal (other employees), and everyone has suppliers whether they be external or internal.

You need to understand your suppliers' work processes as well, because the quality of their input affects your output. Output is any product or service delivered to your customers. Input is what you need in order to produce output, including work environments, materials, and people.

Before you set out to improve a process, it is vital to identify the proper process to improve. You must study the current processes and analyze them to truly understand what it is that's causing the problem. If you don't, you'll end up correcting the wrong thing. This creates rework, saps employee morale, and adds cost.

For example, let's say a credit union has been experiencing a lot of bankruptcy claims. So, the credit union employees form a team to brainstorm possible causes and solutions. The team might come up with a variety of causes: the sponsor company laid-off many workers, an attorney in town placed ads advocating bankruptcy

Instead of understanding and improving the process, management "assumed" that the goal could be achieved and sustained. The fact that the system appeared to be working better reinforced the attitude that it was getting better. What was really happening was something quite different.

"Work is a zero-sum game. There is only so much a worker can do. If management sets artificial goals and people are evaluated on those goals, they will do what it takes to achieve them. However, in a zero-sum game, something has to be given up. Work may not be completed in a quality fashion, workers may compromise their own comfort and morale, some work may be put on hold. At some point the gains will be lost," said Mr. Haefner.

But the organization learned quickly. A quality engineer worked with top management to do some statistical analysis and conducted a blind experiment to see how the ACD was working. The results were interesting. The system had been set up to shift the calls from one group of phone representatives to another at twenty second intervals. So, for example, after a caller waited for twenty seconds, he or she would be shifted to a different set of representatives in order to be helped faster.

This was good logic. But what was not known until the experiment was that when the caller was switched, he or she went to the bottom of the next queue, thus actually waiting longer. Management's new understanding of how the system worked prompted

(continued)

as a viable solution, and it's become so-cially conscionable and legally feasible to declare bankruptcy. Based on these as-sumptions, this credit union team might propose a variety of solutions: launch a massive marketing campaign to educate the public on the ills of bankruptcy and a lobbying crusade to change local laws.

But what if the problem was with the credit union's process, not external influ-ences? Perhaps if this team went back and looked at the loan applications in question, it would find inadequate care had been taken to approve these loans. It might find that the applicants were likely risks for bankruptcy. Perhaps the process allowed especially high-risk applicants to fall through the system and receive loans.

In this case, the way to fix the bank-ruptcy cases was not to run a huge, ex-pensive marketing campaign, but to im-prove the loan process.

more investigation. It found that customers began to anticipate the switches. They became conditioned to hang up the phone just prior to the twenty-second switch. Most customers who hung up did so at eighteen and thirty-eight seconds. They had been perfectly conditioned to unconsciously anticipate the switches.

Now that the system was understood properly, it could be changed correctly. The abandonment rate dropped to below 2%, the lowest in the history of the company.

Did the employees notice that they were handling a much higher volume of work? Not at all. Customers no longer called and recalled. Thus, the phone reps were able to work smoothly and efficiently. They were working smarter, not harder.

TEAM BUILDING

Teams are an integral part of your quality process. They can help you move toward quality in a variety of ways. First of all, teams, by definition, are made up of a variety of people who bring different ideas and experiences to the team; this diversity in perspectives can be used to help solve quality problems.

While a given employee might be able to identify a problem, a single person doesn't usually have enough experience or knowledge to know how to solve it. In a team, many people involved with a work process have the opportunity to voice their opinions and make a quality difference, as well as blend together their skills and experience.

Teams can support each other. During a long project, one person may get tired and discouraged. If many people are working together, chances are that people's work and energies will be spread out, and team members can support each other over the rough spots.

STANDARDIZATION

An important part of quality requires that you consistently meet your members' needs. That consistency is standardization. You should strive to do the same things in the same way all the time, so your members will always receive a proven product.

The point of standardization is to find the best way of doing something, and to do it that same way every time, in order to eliminate "rework" and perform more efficiently. It will also allow you to focus and maximize your skills, rather than having your skills and energies spread out over a variety of work processes that you may not know or understand. Standardization avoids reinventing the wheel.

One example of standardization is new accounts forms. Think of how confusing it would be if everyone had their own form. Or, if member service representatives didn't even use a form, but just asked for information off the top of their heads. Standardization helps eliminate all the problems such a system might cause.

DATA COLLECTION AND STATISTICAL ANALYSIS

Once you have an idea of where you can improve a process, you will need to collect information to back up your assumption. You should collect that information in the form of quantifiable data so you can analyze it statistically later. However, make sure you collect data that is meaningful, because it's easy to end up drowning in data that is useless. When you collect data, follow these steps:

- Form clear goals. You need to have a clear purpose for collecting data, and knowledge of what you hope to accomplish with it.

- Define exactly what kind of data you need. Your definitions should have measurable goals. For example, you may want to measure whether or not your members are getting information on your new loan program in a timely manner. What exactly is a timely manner? Is it a month after it starts? A week? Two days? Or maybe a few hours?

- Map out exactly how you plan to collect the data, what tools you are going to use, and how you are going to analyze and interpret the data.

IPO MODEL

Input	Process	Output
Input What we need to perform our work; the people, information, equipment, supplies, training, procedures.	**Process** What activities are involved in our daily work; work that others need us to do. The definition of a process is when materials or information—*inputs*—are changed or enhanced by an action to produce a different product or result—the *output*.	**Output** What is produced; what service we provide; the final outcome of our work, which could include, for example, a service, product, idea, report, or information.

Supplier

Who provides us with what we need to do our work; can also be internal or external to our organization.

Customer

Who receives our work; can be either internal or external to our organization.

Requirements

What is expected of the work/product/service we provide and receive.

Requirements

What is expected of the work/product/service we provide and receive.

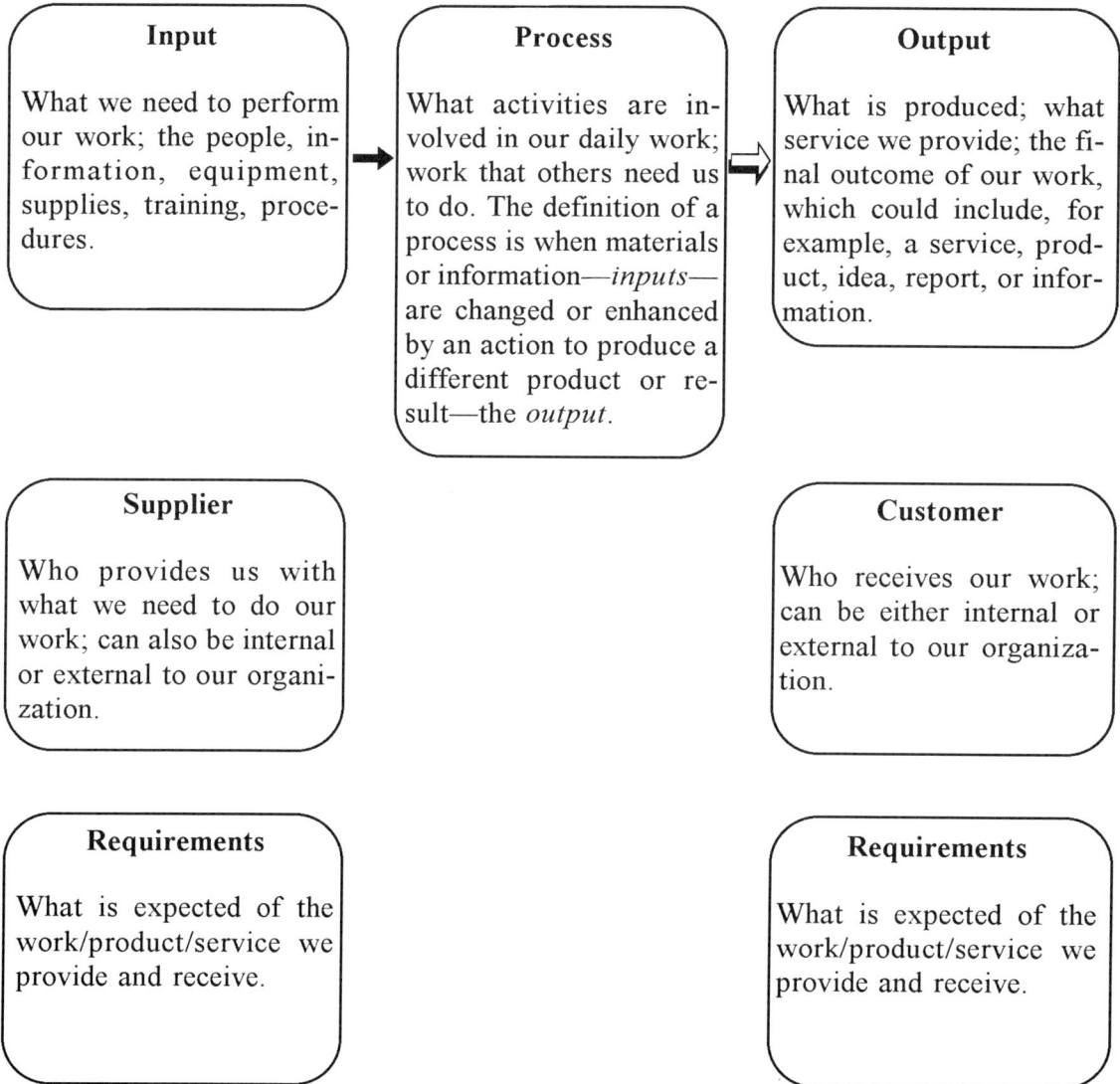

Figure 5. **IPO Model (sample)**

IPO

Suppliers	Process	Customers
Credit Union Management Board of Directors Sponsor Credit Union Staff Illinois Bell "X" Phone Company Members	Answering incoming member calls within one minute.	Credit Union Employees Members Management Board of Directors

Requirements

Trainer
Knowledge of phone system, patient, easy to understand, prepared materials.

Phone Center Representatives
Good attitude, willing to learn, energetic, friendly, courteous, knowledgeable, ability to handle pressure, representative to work on time, adequate staff, online system up and working.

Members
To know account number and know why they are calling.

Board of Directors/Upper Management
Support, supply dependable phone system and tools to perform job properly.

"X-Phone System"
Simple, efficient, reliable, adaptable, state of the art.

Phone/Line/Headsets
Simple, efficient, reliable, adaptable, state of the art.

Phone Directory
Current, complete, and accurate.

Requirements

Minimum hold time (under one minute)
Direct line to Phone Center
Friendly, courteous committed, knowledgeable Phone Center Reps.
Adequate training on phone system
Adequate staff to answer all phone calls
Accurate means to measure hold time of all incoming calls

Output

Calls answered in one minute.

Inputs

Man	*Machine*
Trainer, Phone Center Reps., Members, Management, Board of Directors	Phone/Lines Headsets
Method "X" Phone System	*Materials* Directory Phone List

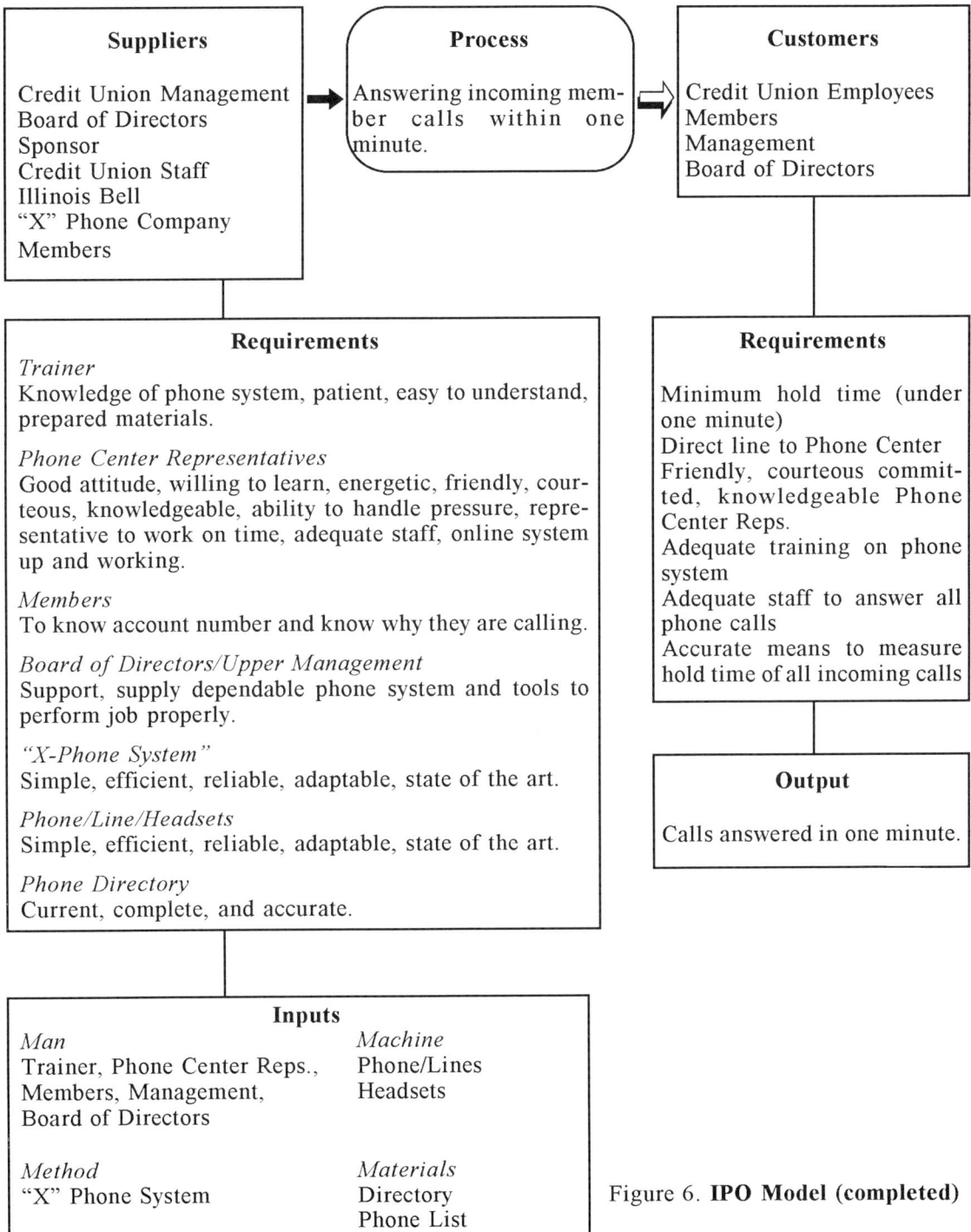

Figure 6. **IPO Model (completed)**

BASIC TOOLS FOR QUALITY IMPROVEMENT

As we stated earlier, tools are the instruments you will use to solve problems. The following list describes some of the many widely known quality tools.

FLOWCHARTS

In order to improve your work processes, you need to determine what is wrong with them. This is where flowcharting can help. Flowcharts are a visual representation of all the steps involved in a process. They help delineate each step in a process and show how the steps relate to each other. Flowcharts can help you uncover holes in the process, as well as unnecessary steps or back loops, bottlenecks, and redundancies.

Make one flowchart that shows how your current process works and another that shows how you want it to work. By comparing the two charts, you can begin to understand how to improve your current process.

CAUSE-AND-EFFECT DIAGRAM

You will find the cause-and-effect diagram helpful when you want to identify the possible causes of a particular outcome. Because it resembles a fish skeleton, you may often hear people call it a "fishbone diagram." The "bones and body" of the diagram represent the causes. They are connected, like the bones of a skeleton, and point to the head, which represents the effect, or the outcome of the causes. The skeletal structure can help you determine the relationship between the causes and the effect.

You'll often use the cause-and-effect diagram to understand problems that you've identified after flowcharting a process. Often, teams brainstorm to organize all the possible causes of a problem. During the brainstorming exercise, each problem becomes the "effect" or head of the skeleton. Team members fill out the skeleton by identifying the possible causes. The skeleton leads to the effect as shown in the figure 8.

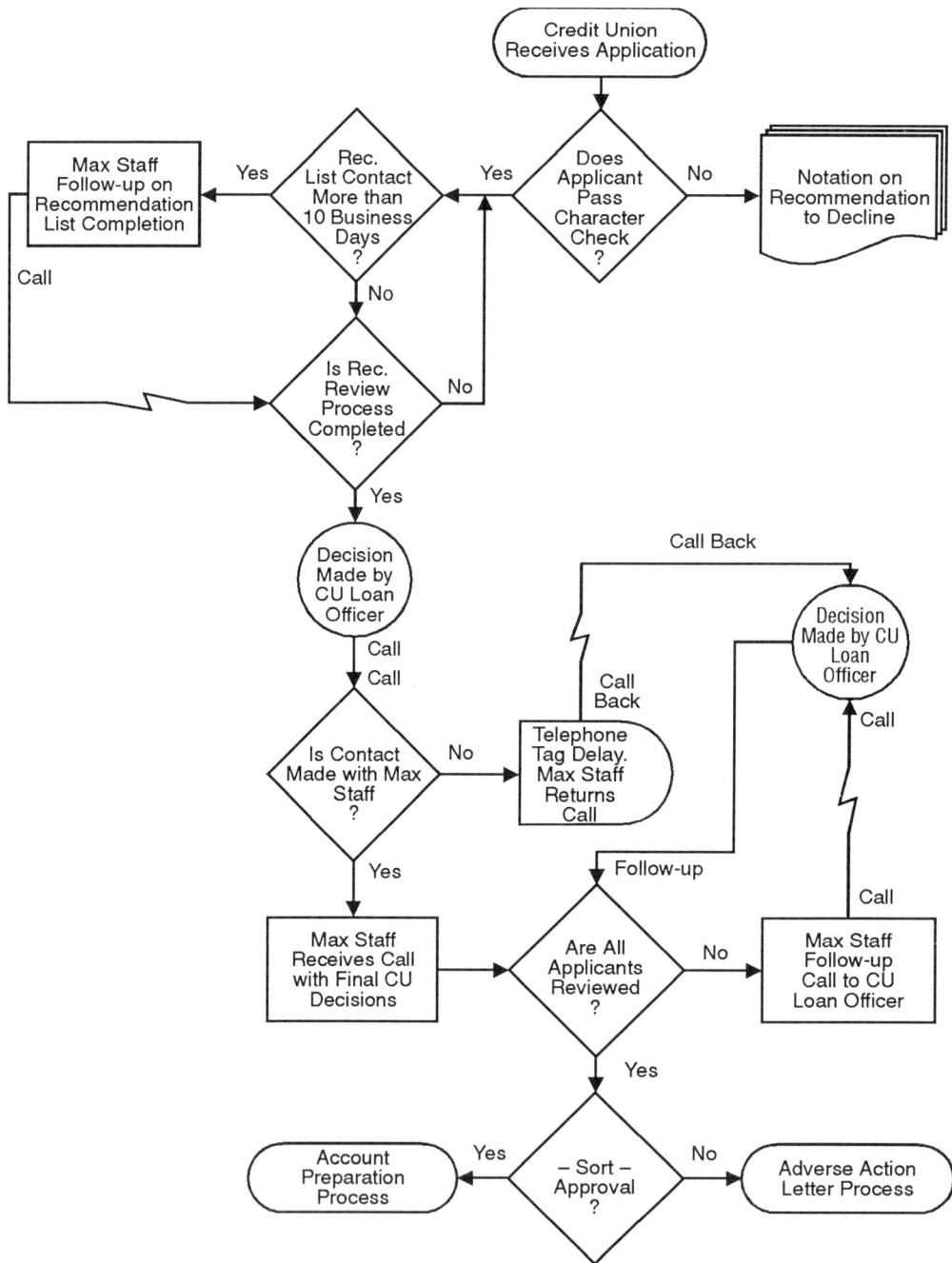

Figure 7: **Flowchart**

Flowcharting Process Brings Measurable Results to Greenway Processing Center

The Greenway Processing Center, a unit within CUNA Service Group's Card Services division, decided to move slowly when it started its TQM initiative. Managers at the card processing facility wanted to improve the simple, everyday process of sending advertising and other informational inserts to members along with their monthly credit card statements. At first glance, the task seemed easy. How complex could stuffing envelopes be?

The center established a process improvement team that explored several options in making the insert process more efficient. One option included creating a new department for managing the process—a costly solution, but the team members thought dedicating more people to the problem would bring improvement.

The team members realized quickly however, that the process was taking on a life of its own when the solution became more complicated than the problem itself. They sought the advice of Joe Haefner, TQM administrator in CUNA & Affiliates Credit Union Card Services. He suggested that Greenway step back from finding a solution and spend time trying to understand the problem.

He suggested making a flowchart to better understand the process. As people on the process improvement team flowcharted each step of the insert process, they found out how complicated it had become. Haefner said, "To our amazement, we had seventy steps. Many of them were cost-added, repetitive, redundant activities. That was the problem."

The flowcharting activity helped the team members identify areas where Greenway was simply making more work for itself. "Right off the bat they were able to subtract five or ten steps before they even gave it much thought," Haefner said. "They simply removed duplicated steps that were unnecessary."

Haefner said Greenway continues to improve the mail insert process. "I think they've created a cost-effective, efficient process that serves the members' needs. They should now be down to twenty steps, maybe twenty-five, at the maximum," Haefner said.

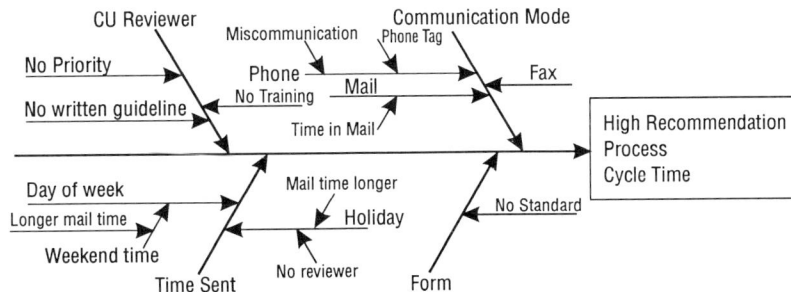

Figure 8. **Cause-and-Effect Diagram**

Team MAX © CSG Card Services Recipient of RIT *USA Today*

TEAM PROGRESS RECORD

TEAM:

DATE:

WEEK	-5	-4	-3	-2	-1	1	2	3	4	5	6	7	8	9	10	11	12	13	14	15
7. CONCLUDE PROJECT — 7.2 DESCRIBE FUTURE PLANS																				
7.1 CHECK PROCESS & RESULTS; DESCRIBE WHAT WAS LEARNED																				
6. STANDARDIZE IMPROVEMENTS — 6.2 STANDARDIZE KEY ITEMS																				
6.1 ESTABLISH CONTROL METHODS — 6.1.2 MONITOR KEY PROCESS CHARACTERISTICS																				
6.1.1 MONITOR KEY QUALITY CHARACTERISTICS																				
5.2 VERIFY THE IMPROVEMENT RESULTS																				
5. VERIFY THE RESULTS — 5.1 IMPLEMENT AT FULL SCALE — 5.1.3 UPGRADE THE PLAN & IMPLEMENT AT FULL SCALE																				
5.1.2 STUDY THE SMALL SCALE IMPLEMENTATION																				
5.1.1 IMPLEMENT ON A SMALL SCALE																				
4. DEVELOP IMPROVEMENTS — 4.2 PLAN, SCHEDULE AND BUDGET THE IMPLEMENTATION																				
4.1 SELECT IMPROVEMENTS — 4.1.2 DETERMINE THE IMPROVEMENTS TO BE MADE																				
4.1.1 GENERATE ALTERNATIVES																				
3.2 VERIFY THE THEORIES WITH DATA — 3.2.3 REPRODUCE PROBLEM TO VERIFY CAUSES																				
3.2.2 INTEGRATE THE INFORMATION COLLECTED																				
3.2.1 COLLECT INFO TO VERIFY ROOT CAUSES																				
3. ANALYZE ROOT CAUSES — 3.1 THEORIES FOR ROOT CAUSES — 3.1.3 PRIORITIZE THEORIES FOR ROOT CAUSES																				
3.1.2 REFINE DIAGRAM OF CAUSES																				
3.1.1 DIAGRAM CAUSE & EFFECT RELATIONSHIP																				
2.2 DETERMINE AND MEASURE STRATEGIES																				
2. OBSERVE THE CURRENT SITUATION — 2.1 INVESTIGATE KEY FEATURES — 2.1.3 VERIFY THEORIES WITH DATA																				
2.1.2 DEVELOP THEORIES FOR KEY FEATURES																				
2.1.1 STUDY HOW WORK IS DONE																				
1.2 STATE THE REASONS FOR WORKING ON THIS THEME																				
1. DETERMINE THE THEME — 1.1 SELECT THE PROJECT THEME — 1.1.4 DETERMINE THEME & MEASURE PROGRESS																				
1.1.3 CLARIFY PROCEDURE & IDENTIFY BOUNDARIES																				
1.1.2 UNDERSTAND THE CUSTOMER PERSPECTIVE																				
1.1.1 IDENTIFY A GENERAL ISSUE																				
0. ORGANIZE THE TEAM — 0.2 FORM THE TEAM																				
0.1 ESTABLISH THE PROJECT IN THE ORGANIZATION																				

Figure 9. **Check Sheet**

Causes are usually grouped into five categories: equipment and machines, people, methods, materials, and environment. You may need to add other categories to this list.

CHECK SHEET

Check sheets are simple ways of collecting data that deal with the question "How often does a certain activity occur?" They provide the hard numbers on which to base your observations.

Check sheets usually look like the example shown on the proceeding page (Figure 9).

Before using a check sheet, decide what event you are observing, and how long you are going to observe it. Make sure you collect the data accurately and honestly.

After you gather the data, you can gain a better understanding of what it means if you display it visually. It is generally best to use a Pareto diagram, histogram, or a run/control chart.

PARETO DIAGRAM

A Pareto diagram displays frequently occurring problems and helps you determine which problems to solve first. The chart was named after the Pareto Prin-

Before Improvement
Pareto Diagram (MAX Application Process)

After Improvement
Pareto Diagram (MAX Application Process)

Figure 10. **Pareto Diagram**

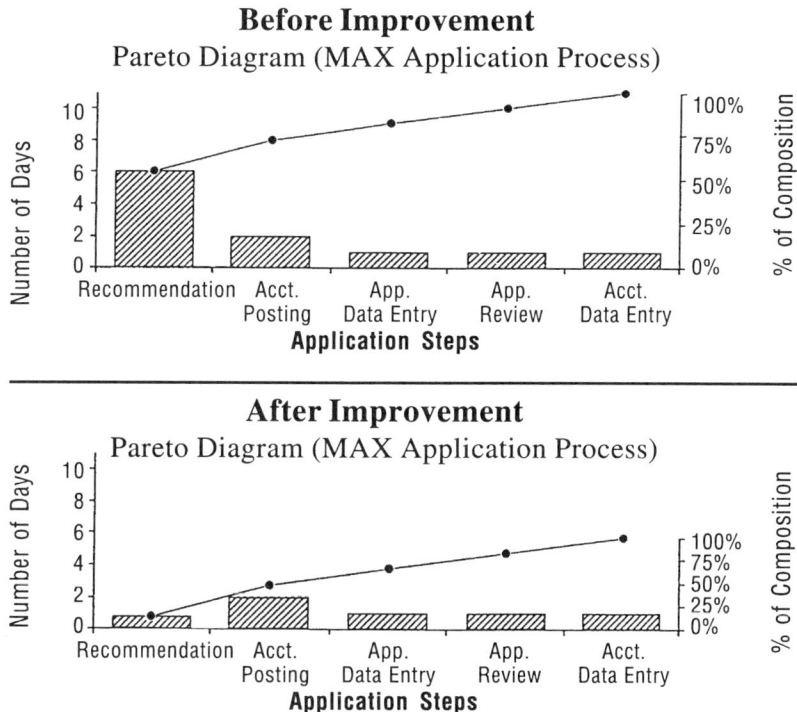

Team MAX© CSG Card Services Recipient of RIT *USA Today*

ciple or the 80/20 rule—80% of the troubles come from 20% of the problems. It's a type of bar chart arranged with the tallest vertical bars on the left and the shortest on the right. The tallest bars are the more important problems. That way, you can see in a glance what you need to work on first. The vertical axis measures frequency, cost, or some other variable. The horizontal axis displays the characteristics of a product or service.

You can use a Pareto diagram at all stages in a project. Use it early to identify the problems, or later to narrow down specific causes.

HISTOGRAM

A histogram is a bar chart, like a Pareto diagram, but instead of showing the variations between different processes, it shows variations in data within the same process. This way you can begin to see where your repeated processes are varying over time. For example, let's say you want to show the number of days it takes your members to receive information on your loan program. Some members may receive their information in two days, while for others it's three days, or four, or five, and so on.

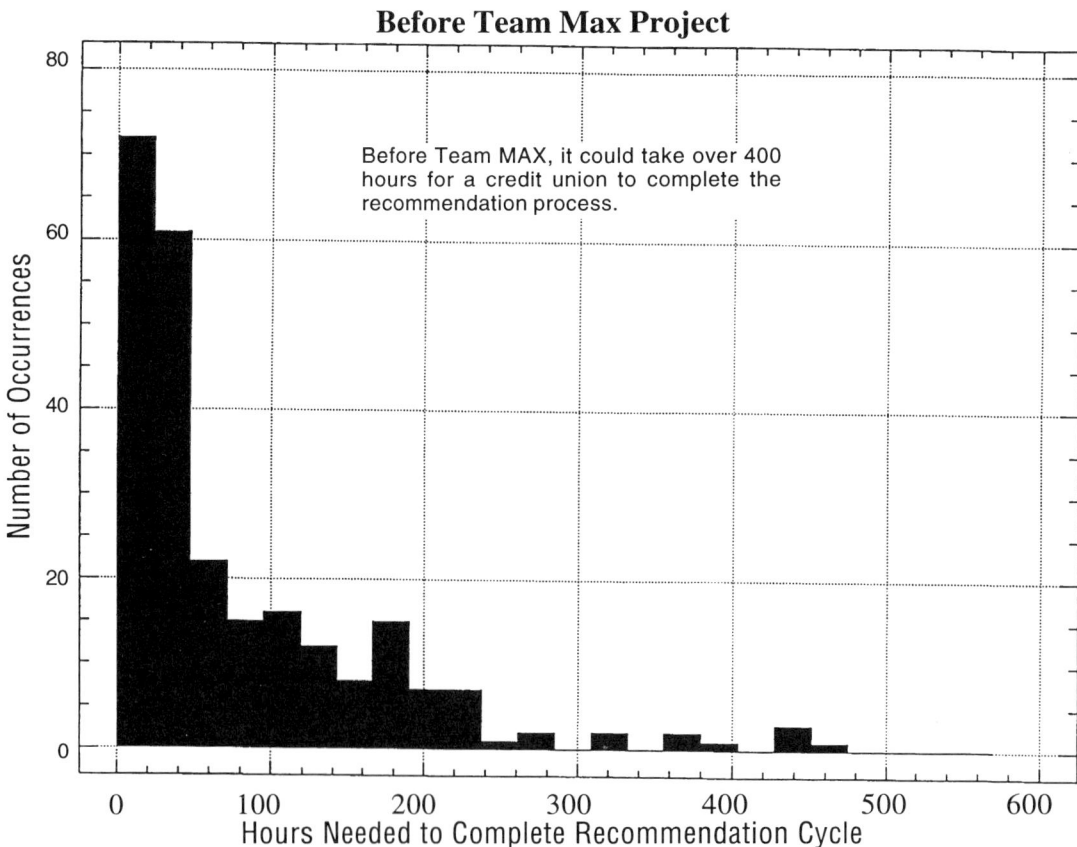

Before Team Max Project

Before Team MAX, it could take over 400 hours for a credit union to complete the recommendation process.

Number of Occurrences (vertical axis)
Hours Needed to Complete Recommendation Cycle (horizontal axis)

Figure 11. **Histogram**

Team MAX© CSG Card Services Recipient of RIT *USA Today*

Look for surprises in the distribution. If something is supposed to be normal or skewed, and it's not, you should ask yourself why.

To construct the horizontal side of the histogram, organize the data into classes. Then, subtract the lowest value from the highest value and divide by the number of classes. The number you calculate represents the width of each class.

SCATTER DIAGRAM

Scatter diagrams indicate a cause and effect relationship between two variables.

They can't identify which variables cause the effect, but they can tell you if a cause and effect relationship exists. Plot the intersection of one variable from the horizontal axis and the other variable from the vertical axis. The tighter the dots appear on the chart, and the more the dots form an upward motion, the more likely a cause and effect relationship is indeed occurring. (When something makes one variable go up, the other variable also goes up.)

You'll need to study the diagram carefully to determine which variable is causing the effect and how strong the relation-

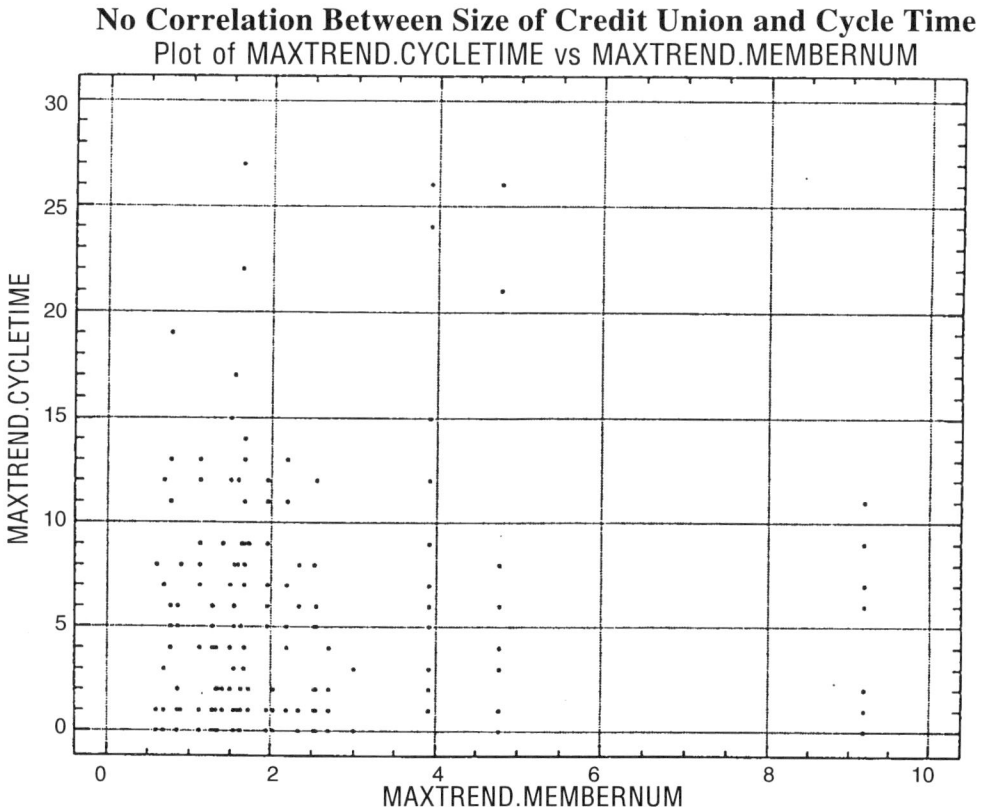

No Correlation Between Size of Credit Union and Cycle Time
Plot of MAXTREND.CYCLETIME vs MAXTREND.MEMBERNUM

Figure 12. **Scatter Diagram**

Team MAX© CSG Card Services Recipient of RIT *USA Today*

ship is. For example, you might want to explore the correlation between the number of errors tellers make when they count their boxes and the number of hours of overtime they work. To plot the variables, you would measure "mistakes made" on the vertical side of the diagram and "overtime hours" on the horizontal side. Each plotted dot would represent a pair of measurements. (For four mistakes and five overtime hours you would plot where those two variables meet.)

RUN CHART

Run charts (otherwise known as line or fever charts) identify trends, patterns, and data variability over time. They indicate when an average is changing over time.

To find a pattern, plot "time" on the horizontal axis and the variable you're measuring on the vertical axis. Because the measurement is based on time, it's important to chart the data in the order in which it occurred.

Project Trend Chart

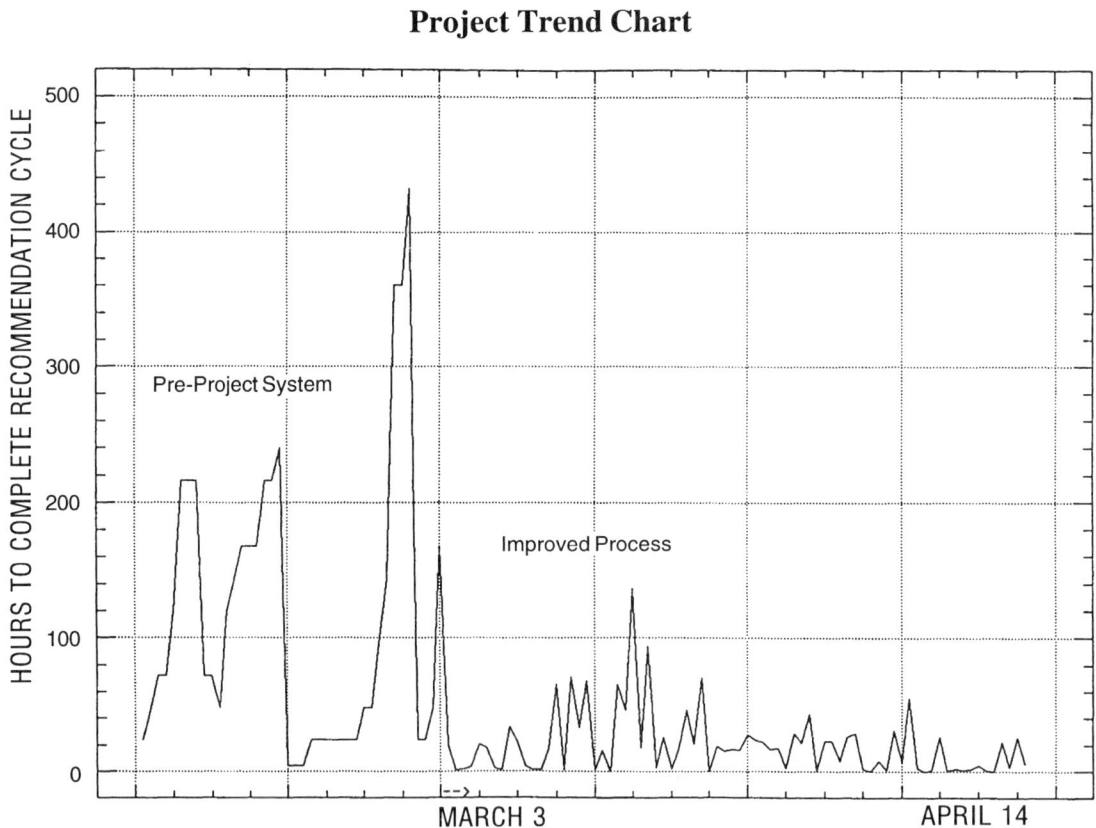

Figure 13. **Run Chart**

Team MAX© CSG Card Services Recipient of RIT *USA Today*

To read a run chart, find the average and draw a straight line across the chart. Count how many dots appear on both sides of the line. You should expect to have an equal number of points above and below the line. If you find more points on one side, it means the average has changed. If this is a good change, you should find out why it changed and make it a permanent part of the process; if not, you should find out how to avoid it. Always investigate any changes in the average.

CONTROL CHART

A control chart is a type of run chart with upper and lower control limits and an average. It helps distinguish between common causes (causes that are built into the process) and special causes (freak

Recommendation Cycle Time Control Chart

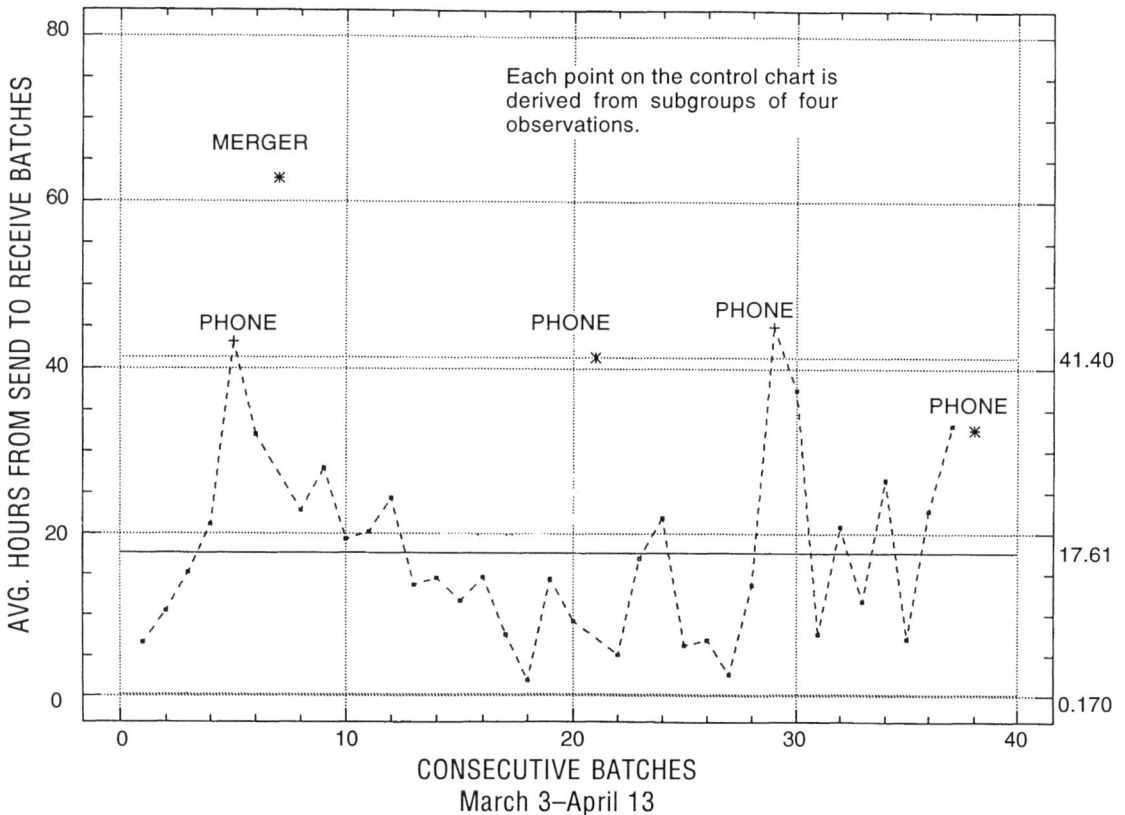

Figure 14. **Control Chart**

accidents that are not inherent in the process, like a citywide black out or flash flood) of the variation in the process. All the special causes need to be eliminated before you can monitor the process. After that, your process is "in control" and you should take random samples to make sure you are not deviating too much from the norm.

Keep in mind that a control chart shows consistency, not a judgment of good or bad. You can have a consistently bad process.

SELECTED ARTICLES

The following articles will help to round out your understanding of total quality management. It's not meant to be an exhaustive list, but a supplement within this introductory "reader." Some of the articles describe how quality is applied in the service sector. Some reflect the experience of financial institutions, including credit unions. Others speak to the training component in TQM. Taken together, they're just a very small sampling of what's available from business and trade publications. We hope they kindle your interest in keeping up with the latest developments in total quality management!

Principles of Total Quality

Stephen R. Covey

Stephen Covey's best-seller, "7 Habits of Highly Effective People," sold one million copies and is still going strong. This is an excerpt from his latest book, in which he tells how to achieve personal fulfillment and professional success through principle-centered leadership.

The paradigm of total quality is continuous improvement. No person or company should be content to stay where they are, no matter how successful they now seem to be. And very few people or companies could possibly be content with the *status quo* if they were regularly receiving accurate feedback on their performance from their stakeholders.

Total quality is an expression of the need for continuous improvement in four areas: 1) personal and professional development; 2) interpersonal relations; 3) managerial effectiveness; and 4) organizational productivity.

Personal and professional development. You and I are the keys to total quality. It's what I call an inside-out approach to quality. Inside out

means to start first with yourself—your paradigms, character, and motives. This approach often requires personal change—not personnel changes.

W. Edwards Deming has said that about 90 percent of the problems in organizations are general problems (bad systems); only about ten percent are specific problems with people. Many managers misinterpret such data, supposing that if they then correct the structure and systems (programs), the problems with people (programmers) will go away. The reverse is actually true: if you correct the ten percent first, the other problems will go away.

Continuous improvement basically means you never are content with something being half-right. Your customers certainly won't be content. And if you are getting accurate feedback from them, you will be motivated and challenged to improve.

Interpersonal. Total quality on an interpersonal level means making constant deposits into the emotional bank accounts of others. It is con-

tinually building good will and negotiating in good faith, not in fear. If you create an expectation of continuous product or service improvement but fail to deliver on that expectation, you will see a buildup of fear and negative forecasting.

A corporate culture, like the human body, is an ecosystem of interdependent relationships, and these must be balanced synergistically and based on trust to achieve quality.

Managerial. Managerial quality is basically nurturing win-win performance and partnership agreements—making sure they are "in sync" with what is happening inside that person and what is happening inside the business.

Win-win thinking creates teamwork. Win-lose thinking creates rivalry.

We need internal unity to get win-win cooperation, loyalty to the mission, constancy of purpose.

Most people search for quality in techniques, practices, and processes; they don't realize that quality requires a whole different explanation of the role of management.

People must know that they are being managed by principles and entitled to due process.

Management's job is empowerment. If you want to influence and empower people, first recognize that they are resourceful and have vast untapped capability and potential. Understand their purpose, point of view, language, concerns, customers, boss. Be loyal. Maintain credibility.

Organizational. Proactivity is the essence of real leadership. Every great leader has a high level of proactive energy and vision—a sense that I am not a product of my culture, my conditioning, and the conditions of my life; rather, I am a product of my value system, attitudes, and behavior—and those things I control.

I recommend that every organization develop a stakeholder information system—a feedback system or database on what shareholders, customers, employees, communities, suppliers, distributors, and other parties want and expect.

I also suggest that every organization develop synergistic relationships with customers and suppliers. There is a place for competition, but it's not in areas where you need to cooperate.

Total quality is a principle-centered approach that has come out of the best the world has produced. In our training, we emphasize the human side more than the technical side because we believe that the origin and essence of total quality is empathy with customers, empathy with their motives and buying habits.

Everything is guided by feedback from customers—both internal and external—and from other stakeholders. The key to total quality is to listen to your stakeholders, to seek first to understand, then to be understood.

DEMING'S 14 POINTS

APPLIED TO SERVICE

Lots of service operations talk a good game, but they lag behind manufacturers in adopting quality as a way of life.

By Ronald W. Butterfield

Since the 1950s, W. Edwards Deming has been a familiar name in Japan. Deming, and the famous 14 Points that summarize the core of his philosophy, are considered largely responsible for Japanese industry's post-World War II recovery and rise to dominance in world markets.

But most U.S. manufacturers ignored Deming's work until around 1980. By then, thanks to severe competition, many were at death's door. Indeed, some had already died and disappeared. They were the ones that assumed there would always be a market for anything American industry produced. Instead, ongoing improvement in cost, quality and productivity had become critical to survival. For those who would listen and were willing to make the commitment, Deming had answers.

The service sector of the U.S. economy stands at a similar crossroad today. In the financial industry for example, deregulation opened the field to fresh competition in the '80s. Today, increasing global competition in everything from banking to credit cards means domestic organizations need to develop a quality edge—quickly. Service industry leaders are familiar with Deming and his 14 Points, but many decline to adopt them because, they contend, "service is different from manufacturing."

The real reason may be that most service managers are so busy fighting fires they don't have time to reflect. They simply don't think about how to translate Deming's concepts into the language of service or to incorporate his principles into their corporate cultures. And even if they want to, few resources are available to guide them. Most quality consultants have a manufacturing background. They approach quality concepts from that perspective, and then add, "Of course, all these things are equally applicable to service businesses."

But the 14 Points do apply to the service industry. Reluctant managers will ask: "Why go to all that effort? Why not just keep telling our people how important quality is and encouraging them to keep doing their best?" According to Mary Walton's 1986 book, *The Deming Management Method*, Deming's answer to such questions is straightforward: "Everyone doing his best is not the answer. Everyone *is* doing his best. It is necessary that people understand the reason for the transformation that is necessary for survival. Moreover, there must be consistency of understanding and of effort. There is no substitute for knowledge."

When it comes to managing quality, manufacturers have a significant jump on service organizations. Some service firms talk a good game about quality and busily measure performance indicators, but there's little evidence that many are serious about adopting quality as a

way of life.

Here is an attempt at a service-oriented interpretation of Deming's 14 Points. It may shed some light on how to make quality an integral part of the service business.

1. *Create constancy of purpose toward improvement of product and service.* To maintain constancy of purpose, we must concentrate on the interplay among three basic elements: unit cost, which must be kept as low as possible while maintaining objectives of accuracy and timeliness; customers' needs, wants and satisfaction; and employees, who must understand the organization's mission, and then be properly trained and given the tools necessary to fulfill that mission.

Suppose you manage the policyholder service operation for an insurance company. What does constancy of purpose imply for you? First, you must recognize that your sole purpose is to serve the owners of the policies sold by your company. To serve suggests that you are meeting specific needs. Therefore, constancy of purpose means you continuously strive to understand the needs, expectations and satisfaction levels of your policyholders. You even try to anticipate their needs.

You might, for example, install a computer-driven audio response service to give policyholders basic information such as cash values, policy-loan balances or policy-loan interest paid for the year. Not only does such a service satisfy specific customer needs, it lowers unit cost per contact because no human effort is required to answer the inquiry. It also benefits employees because they no longer have to handle such routine calls.

Constancy of purpose means that your organization's customers, people and unit costs form the framework for management decision making. It requires vision and leadership.

2. *Adopt a new philosophy.* With the second point, Deming is suggesting that management must undergo a radical transformation to maintain the company's viability in the global marketplace. Quality must become the preeminent concern. Errors, poor materials and rework must be eliminated throughout the production system or service delivery process.

Consider your company's suppliers. If you purchase mailing lists from a variety of vendors, for example, you know some are much more accurate than others. Point 2 suggests that if one of your people notices that a particular vendor's lists are chronically inaccurate, it should be brought to management's attention. It should not be ignored or accepted as normal. Likewise, management should raise the issue with the vendor so the vendor can try to improve.

3. *Cease dependence on mass inspection.* You cannot inspect quality into any product or service. When you throw out or rework a defective item, you are not concentrating on quality improvement—nor are you improving unit cost. Therefore, Deming says, stop relying on mass inspections of the final result of a process (the finished product). Rather, concentrate on improving the process itself so that you'll prevent errors from occurring in the first place.

Let's apply this principle to the real estate loan department of a bank. One of its functions is to prepare documents for signature by the buyer and seller, and to file them with the Registrar of Deeds. Suppose mortgage and escrow-payment amounts are frequently typed incorrectly by the typing pool. Rather than going back to the source of the problem, loan officers simply toss out the forms with

> When it comes to managing quality, manufacturers have a significant jump on service organizations.

the incorrect numbers on them and have their own secretaries retype them correctly. What happens? Errors continue to show up and unit cost per loan package increases significantly.

If quality and productivity are important to this bank, what should it do? Hiring people to inspect all of the work coming out of the typing pool is not the answer. A better solution is to go back and follow documents through the entire process to find out why the payment amounts are incorrect. Maybe some of the loan officers are providing the wrong information. Maybe the errors are due simply to haste and carelessness in the document-preparation area. The bank must find the cause of the problem and fix it, not just nurse the symptoms.

4. *End the practice of awarding business on the basis of price tag.* We have been in the habit of giving business to the lowest bidder

for too long. Purchasing managers have to reassess their roles and responsibilities. They have a key role to play in the quality improvement process. They must understand when and how the materials and supplies they order will be used.

Even something as simple as pin-feed billing forms requires careful scrutiny of vendors. The paper stock must meet stated standards. Printed forms should not be delivered until properly cured. Perforations and printed sections should be correctly placed. Lack of attention to these factors can cause jamming, wrinkling, smearing and misalignment when statements are being processed.

Standards and requirements for every item or service purchased from vendors should be established and then followed to the letter. Nothing less is acceptable. It won't be long before you realize the value of a single supply source and a long-term relationship with your vendor.

5. *Improve constantly and forever the system of production and service.* At the beginning of any quality improvement effort it is fairly easy to realize major gains in accuracy, timeliness and productivity by using simple sampling and Pareto analysis. Gradually, the primary causes of errors are eliminated and the process is brought into statistical control. But a process that is in statistical control in not error-free.

Let's say you manage an area that handles correspondence from customers. When you start a quality improvement program, you'll probably begin by sampling recently closed correspondence files. If the sampling is done correctly, you'll quickly find out which employees are making the most errors in correspondence and what types of errors they are making most frequently. You can take action—retraining, coaching, etc.—to bring the process into statistical control. But your job isn't finished. In fact, you're just beginning.

The real work involves looking for ways to improve the process itself. Perhaps work flow can be improved, and the total time required to process incoming items can be reduced. Maybe some parts of the process can be automated, eliminating certain opportunities for error. The customer correspondence unit, for example, could put its most frequently used replies on computer so that letters are generated simply by entering the appropriate code.

6. *Institute training on the job.* Too often workers learn their jobs from other workers who are poorly trained or from inadequate printed instructions. Many workers don't know what constitutes a good job or a bad job.

Training is not a fringe benefit for employees. It's not something you do only when you are in danger of failing to meet your production quota or quality standards. And it's not something you do only when you have time. Train-

---

Find the cause
of the problem and
fix it;
don't just nurse
the symptoms

---

ing must be a planned part of the system or process. You cannot produce a quality product or deliver a quality service without it. The bottom line directly reflects training quality.

Managers responsible for processing customer payments should think about training needs *before* their people fail to meet productivity goals or they're deluged with encoding errors. Training should

begin the first day for each new employee.

7. *Institute leadership.* As Deming says, leaders should aim to help people and machines do a better job.

Since it's management's job to provide leadership, managers must work continually to uncover barriers to pride of workmanship. Employees know exactly what the barriers are: pressure to meet deadlines without concern for quality, an overriding emphasis on numbers, inadequate tools for doing the job, continual rework of items that are in error and so on.

Deming suggests that typical supervisors allow these barriers to exist because they don't know the job and aren't interested in learning it. Workers realize this and are reluctant to bring up problems they see.

The customer-service people in a commercial bank often use microfiche containing customer accounts if an on-line computer system is not available. Suppose the quality of the microfiche is poor, which makes some of the data difficult to read and results in frequent errors. If this barrier is to be eliminated, workers should feel free to bring the problem to their supervisor's attention.

The supervisor should feel equally free to take the problem to management, which must act quickly and decisively to correct the situation.

8. *Drive out fear.* Eliminating fear in the workplace is something we hear very little about. Perhaps fear at work is so commonplace that we just accept it as normal and think little of it. We have not recognized fear for what it is: a primary cause of quality and productivity problems.

The types of fears Deming addresses include fear of asking questions, fear of expressing ideas, fear of asking for further instructions, fear of mentioning that equipment is not working properly and fear of raising issues about working conditions.

According to Deming, the cost of fear in the workplace is appalling. Consider the operator of an embossing machine in a credit-card processing center. Volume for the month is heavy, far above what was forecast. The pressure is on to get production up. The operator has noticed that the plastic card-feed mechanism on the embossing machine is occasionally malfunctioning. But because of the pressure to produce, he says nothing to his supervisor for fear he will be blamed for the resulting backlogs if he

shuts down the machine for repairs. Two days later a major problem develops and the feed mechanism breaks down altogether. Because of the failure to perform preventive maintenance early on, the embossing machine is down for three days rather than for what would have been a three- to four-hour repair job.

9. *Break down barriers between departments.* The point here is simple, yet it is frequently overlooked even by the most experienced managers. An organization cannot run at optimum efficiency if the right hand doesn't know what the left hand is doing. Each area should be aware of how its output affects other areas as well as customers. Each area should be responsible for alerting others to any problems coming their way.

Lack of communication between the marketing department and the customer-contact functions is a typical problem. Marketing develops a new product, service or promotional campaign without getting any input from the people who deal directly with customers every day. No one thinks to ask them how they think customers will react to the product or what kind of impact a new promotional campaign will have on their work load. Sometimes marketing will offer a new ser-

vice to customers without even informing the front-line employees who are supposed to provide it. The first time the poor front-liner hears of the new two-for-one policy is when a customer is standing there angrily demanding number two.

If optimal use of all organizational resources is the goal, all departments must communicate constantly on both a formal and informal basis.

10. *Eliminate slogans, exhortations and targets asking for zero defects and new levels of productivity.* With Point 10, Deming raises an interesting issue that contradicts the views of many management consultants. He tells us to get rid of slogans, banners, buttons and balloons in the workplace. Forget about setting productivity targets for work groups and posting daily, weekly and monthly progress reports. Forget about zero-defects programs and having people sign their work.

All of these efforts are aimed at motivating people to work faster and produce more. According to Deming, they not only don't work, they actually have a negative impact on productivity and quality.

A payment-processing area can illustrate this point. Assume these employees use video display terminals to key in payments. Also assume many of these terminals are old and their screens are difficult to read. If employees are asked to improve their productivity by 10 percent, imagine their response when management's only contribution is to plaster the place with banners proclaiming, "Increase productivity!" or "Do it right the first time!"

Sure it sounds ridiculous. Yet how many times have you seen it happen?

Management's job is to show people how to do their work more accurately and efficiently. To do so, they must provide the proper tools and training required to meet quality and productivity objectives.

Certainly we ought to have numerical goals, but they do not have to be the focal point of the improvement efforts communicated to employees. Instead, we need to work with individuals to help them set their own goals and then integrate those personal goals with the organization's overall goal.

It's all one more way of saying: If we want improvement, we have to lead with actions, not with words.

11. *Eliminate work standards that prescribe numerical quotas. Substitute leadership.* Theoretically, productivity standards are established for the work force so that management meets its output goals. The problem with such quotas and standards is that they are based on averages, which means that half of the people fail to reach standard. This emphasis on productivity rates is ultimately detrimental to morale and to the bottom line. Shoddy performance and poor workmanship are allowed to slip by because of the urgent need to produce.

Front-line employees
know more
than their supervisors
and managers
give them credit for.

The key to productivity and quality improvement is to look for differences in performance and to create an atmosphere of receptivity to new ideas and recognition. An effective productivity standard should be developed and communicated so that everyone knows acceptable standards of quality.

A typical airline reservation center demonstrates this point. If each customer-service representative is asked to handle 20 calls per hour without exception, what may happen? The reps may find themselves cutting a customer short or giving incomplete information in order to meet the productivity standard. If this happens too often, the reps know the job is not being done as it should be and begin to take less pride in their work. The quality of service deteriorates even further, and customer complaints begin to rise.

A good manager will recognize that quality must be an integral part of a service standard. It's more profitable to take a little longer to handle a customer's inquiry properly the first time than it is to spend time calling the customer back. A good manager also will recognize the value of customer-service representatives who are proud of the quality of service they provide.

12. *Remove barriers that rob hourly workers of their right to pride of workmanship.* We touched on this before, under the leadership heading in Step 7. Front-line employees know more than their supervisors and managers give them credit for. Most employees realize that improvements in quality also lead to improvements in productivity. But management frequently places roadblocks in the way of such improvement.

If you ask them, employees will tell you what these roadblocks are. They'll often say they don't know what is expected of them. What is acceptable and what is not changes from one day to the next, depending on the pressure to produce. Employees get little feedback on their performance until review time rolls around and then, of course, it's too late for them to do anything about it.

Management must take the time to understand what hinders people's work. That means asking several questions: Do employees understand what their jobs are? Do they know what level of work is acceptable? Have they been adequately trained? Is the equipment they use in good condition? Are they getting the assistance they need from management? Is there an effective way for them to report problems or suggestions? If so, is prompt action taken to resolve them?

13. *Institute a vigorous program of education and self-improvement.* As a company makes progress in quality and productivity improvement, two types of training needs will arise. First, as productivity improves, the number of employees required to produce the same results will decline. Surplus people must be trained for other positions within the company. (If you expect employees to play an effective role in the improvement process, no one should lose his or her job because of productivity gains.)

You also will need to train selected managers and workers in the fundamentals of statistical quality control. Techniques such as Pareto analysis, for example, allow you to discover the most common errors in a billing operation. Without employees who have a thorough understanding of sampling techniques, control charts, Pareto analysis and so on, further improvement will be limited.

14. *Everybody in the company must work to accomplish the transformation.* Quality must be given equal status with all the other operations in the organization. Without senior management involvement and commitment, improvement efforts will fail.

Top management must appropriate and allocate the resources needed for this effort. Executives must act as quality spokespersons for the organization and make their commitment clear to all employees. Quality must be managed with the same emphasis that financial management receives.

There you have Deming's management philosophy in a nutshell. For those of us involved in training, the challenge is to take the time to understand Deming's work as it applies to our industry and to develop a way to transfer this knowledge to management and employees at all levels as quickly as possible.

Deming's 14 Points apply equally to manufacturing and service management. It's time for those of us in service industries to carry the message into the field. Our friends in manufacturing have already shown us what will happen if we fail to take action. It's not a pretty sight.

Ronald W. Butterfield is a quality and productivity improvement consultant with Management Dynamics, a consulting company in Sioux Falls, SD.

Away from the factory floor, the success stories are few and far between.
Why do service workers get bogged down in quality campaigns?
Maybe there's a faster, better way.

HOW TO IMPROVE QUALITY IF YOU'RE
NOT
IN MANUFACTURING

BY GARY K. JOHNSON AND ROLAND A. DUMAS

Everyone talks quality these days. And that's just not a cliche. *The Quality Observer* reported in April that 76 percent of all companies responding to one 1992 study claimed quality improvement as a key corporate goal.

But another recent study—described in the same article, and typical of current literature on the subject—indicates that organizations are finding it a whole lot easier to talk about quality goals than to achieve them. In interviews with companies that have begun quality-improvement drives, researchers found that more than two-thirds "have failed or not succeeded."

In May, *The Wall Street Journal* put the problem in perspective with a story headlined, "Quality Programs Show Shoddy Results." In September, *Newsweek* ran a similar report.

Companies have become great at drawing up quality-improvement plans, but may not be very good at executing them—at least, not in ways that really appear to strengthen the business. The problem is especially acute when it comes to applying quality methods to jobs that are not directly involved with manufacturing: jobs in companies or departments engaged in sales, merchandising, law, health care, accounting, personnel, insurance, design,

security, food service, finance, administration—the list is enormous.

In fact, if we continued that list, eventually it would include an astounding 85 percent of all jobs, according to Commerce Department statistics in the most recent edition of *Statistical Abstract of the U.S.*

In manufacturing companies, a quality-improvement drive that produces excellent results on the factory floor will often fail to "transfer" to other departments. One appliance maker, for instance, reduced production defects dramatically, but couldn't get its orders processed and shipped on time to meet the

---

retailers' advertised specials. The problem persisted no matter how "involved" everyone became in the total quality process.

In the service sector, meanwhile, many corporate leaders have seen the value of quality-improvement concepts and philosophies, but most find it appallingly difficult to apply the approaches espoused. Company after company tries to emulate the world-class manufacturers only to find that the techniques just don't seem to fit retailing or accounting or whatever. Why not?

THE MANUFACTURING MODEL

Why are North American firms bogged down in quality drives that seem to be going nowhere? What does it take to achieve the results we want, need and swear by before customers go away, employees tire out and management gives up?

Some executives accept disappointing results—for a time—as a natural consequence of change. A CEO will be told that his corporate culture must be completely transformed to set the stage for true quality improvement. For a while, he'll buy it. He'll wait while the organization gets up to speed, building a huge new infrastructure that will allow the quality miracle to occur. But this process may take so long that it stretches the patience of customers, employees—and the board of directors—to the breaking point. Thus, Florida Power & Light, the first non-Japanese company ever to win Japan's Deming Award for quality, stumbles on the bottom line and is forced to reorganize.

The current quality-improvement fervor draws its fundamental energy from successes in manufacturing's quest to turn out better products. Nonmanufacturing endeavors—including "pure services" such as hospitality or health care—have tried to emulate these successes using manufacturing methods.

But there are some distinct differences between a manufactured product and a service. A product—a CD player, for example—is *repetitively produced* to meet *clear specifications* with *rigorous numerical tolerances*. Any deviation can be measured, plotted and isolated. The inspected CD player can then be shelved and inventoried.

Figure 1.
TRADITIONAL QUALITY APPROACH
Generalized

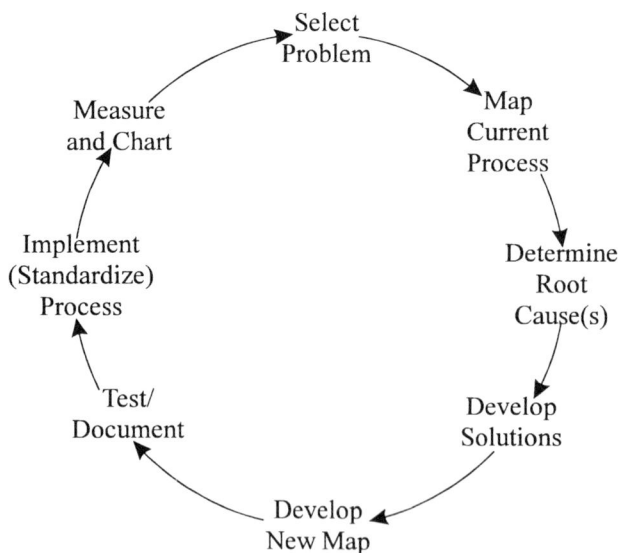

Individual customers seem almost insignificant in the face of the grand corporate plan—even when the plan is officially dedicated to pleasing the customer.

Nonmanufacturing outcomes are fundamentally different. Buy an insurance policy, and the only time you know if and how well it works is when you make a claim. Certainly there is an infrastructure in place to sell the insurance, invest the money and pay the policyholder later. Yet the actual service—what the customer has paid for—is produced and consumed at the same "moment." There is no opportunity to inspect or delay delivery, except in the presence of the waiting customer.

In the quest for results, such obvious differences between manufacturing and nonmanufacturing outputs have been largely ignored. The manufacturing model represents a successful attempt at getting what all are seeking—quality improvement. Therefore, management has reasoned, the generalized manufacturing model (Figure 1) must fit all human endeavor. It should put the quality principles to work everywhere, moving everyone

along to better, brighter and more competitive results.

In the real world, those results are elusive.

WHERE COMPANIES GO WRONG

The success of Japanese companies showed North America and the world a way back to quality—from a manufacturing perspective. Companies everywhere seek continuous improvement (called *kaizen* by the Japanese) and ever-higher quality by isolating defects.

In the face of competitive threats, and in light of the very real benefits of attention to quality, new techniques have sprouted like bean stalks. But most of them are statistical approaches. They are manufacturing-oriented attempts to further quantify quality. Not surprisingly, many organizations have come to define quality in terms of deviation from established numerical norms or specifications.

This is a crucial misstep. Most nonmanufacturing jobs (and again, that term refers to 85 percent of all jobs) do not have the clear, simplified outcomes—the specifications—of manufactured products. Nor do they have the certainty of pre-existing physical measurements that determine whether a product meets those specifications.

Nonmanufacturing tasks *can* have such specifications. The key question is, what are they and how are they determined?

In the manufacturing model, if the product does not fall consistently within specific tolerances, it does not meet quality standards. The moment that happens, we have discovered a problem to deal with. In that light, it makes sense that the traditional quality-improvement cycle begins with *identifying a problem*.

In the nonmanufacturing world—not previously blessed with concrete specifications—

to start by identifying problems can lead to a well-intentioned wild goose chase. Without specifications of what you have committed to supply to a customer, how do you know when it's not being done? Your only evidence will be anecdotal.

Suppose a restaurant chain resolves to improve quality to stay competitive. Following the first step of the traditional (manufacturing) model, management identifies a possible problem that keeps people away: taking too long to deliver food to the customer. To cure the problem, the chain invests time and money to set up a program to monitor how long it takes to deliver each item. Later, however, management discovers that the major cause of customer dissatisfaction and lost business is not delivery time at all. The service problem is actually twofold: Waiters take too long to *initiate* service, then deliver the wrong order half the time because menu items are similar and poorly labeled. Identifying the wrong problem in this case results in lost time, wasted resources and frustration. In an extreme case, the business might even fail, having waited too long to figure out and respond to the customers' real expectations.

LOSING THE WAY

It's becoming a common story: The service organization starts off seeking quality improvement by slavishly following the manufacturing model. The work force gets deeply involved in the quality campaign, but that involvement consists of solving arbitrary problems without benefit of appropriate specifications. Employees waste most of their energy on incidental problems, rather than fundamental system problems that will make a difference. Everyone struggles dutifully

to post and track all sorts of data about these alleged problems. People tire of the effort. Daily work suffers.

Meanwhile, customers—confused and ignored—defect because the organization has become too busy to meet their needs and expectations. After all, individual customers seem almost insignificant in the face of the grand corporate plan—even when the plan is officially dedicated to pleasing the customer. The charts and graphs and team meetings take on a life of

Figure 2.
NONMANUFACTURING APPROACH

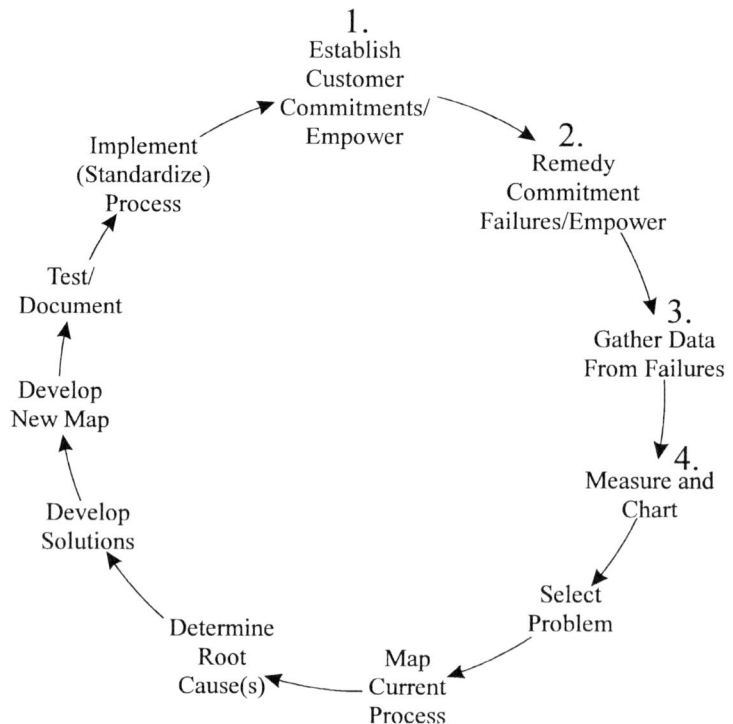

During the data-gathering process every effort has gone into serving customers to the level of your written commitments.

their own, and everyone forgets that handling the needs of customers is the basis of all enterprise. Without customers, everyone's out of business. This is true whether you call them customers, clients, patients, policyholders, taxpayers or constituents.

The manufacturing model of quality improvement addresses the end user only indirectly, by emphasizing measurable product quality. As consultant Karl Albrecht noted in the May issued of *Quality Digest*, "If you examine carefully the work of the three best-known quality thinkers—W. Edwards Deming, Joseph M. Juran and Philip Crosby—you will see that the whole focus of their attention was on processes for manufacturing products...."

In nonmanufacturing jobs, what's really needed is to establish valid customer-based specifications by which real quality problems can be identified and fixed. And do all this while meeting the needs of present customers.

WHAT TO DO?

There is a rapid-deployment methodology that allows nonmanufacturing organizations to do just that—an approach that can set them on the path of continuous improvement with immediate results. This version of a quality-improvement process resembles the manufacturing model but adds four additional steps (Figure 2).

1. *Get specifications by creating customer commitments.* In manufacturing, specifications indicate acceptable outcomes. Customer commitments serve the same purpose for nonmanufacturing jobs; they are statements of outcomes expected in nonmanufacturing situations. These commitments are designed to satisfy customers' needs and expectations, written to include "a little something extra" to distinguish our service from others. For example, an accounting department could commit to supply needed information to the sales department in an

easy-to-read graphic form—with explanatory notes—instead of just raw numbers.

Customer commitments are based on everyone's inherent general understanding of customer needs, combined with actual knowledge of what the customer wants. For commitments to be as effective as specifications, all employees must know who their customers are; the specific expectations of these customers must be written down; and employees must be empowered by management to do whatever is necessary to meet these expectations.

2. *Keep your customers by remedying commitment failures.* The systems for delivering the level of quality specified in your commitments are probably not yet perfected or standardized. So it's natural for commitment failures to occur. You'll need to gather data in order to identify and correct the problems behind these failures. But while this data gathering goes on, customers must be taken care of.

To be able to fix a commitment failure—that is, a customer problem—on the spot, you must anticipate possible failures and devise suitable remedies. These plans must be mapped out in advance, written down and agreed to by management. And the work force must be empowered to act on them.

For example, a service representative at a car dealership has a written commitment to ensure that every auto-repair appointment is completed on the day promised. He's empowered to make this commitment by his boss, the service manager. As a remedy in the event of failure, the rep is authorized to arrange for a mechanic to work overtime to complete any unfinished repairs.

Studies by Technical Assistance Research Programs (TARP), a Washington, D.C., consulting firm, confirm that you can keep 98 percent of your customers if you fix their problems immediately.

3. *Gather data to find the real problems.* You need to identify system problems and assign priorities to them, so you can concentrate on the 20 percent of problems that cause 80 percent of all commitment failures.

By calculating the cost of lost customers and the cost of fixing each service failure, you can measure the real cost of every failure to meet a customer commitment. By tracking the frequency of each type of failure, and multiplying by the predetermined costs for that incident, you have concrete numbers that show the impact of failing to meet each kind of customer commitment.

Now you can "talk from data" in nonmanufacturing functions, instead of depending on anecdotes to decide what's important. In effect, you've got specifications: A commitment failure is analogous to a deviation from standard in a manufacturing setting.

Suppose a furniture company gathers data about each customer commitment failure that occurs. The company expects to confirm its belief that the biggest problem involves goods marred in transit. Instead it finds that the most frequent failure, and the costliest overall, lies in delivering to customers' homes. Making deliveries at the time requested is far more crucial—at least, initially—to keeping and building a solid customer base.

4. *Measure and chart to establish bases for improvement.* The initial "fix" of a customer commitment failure (paying that mechanic to work overtime, for example) is really just a "workaround" to keep customers satisfied. Once you have gathered good data, you can effectively attack the real problems behind commitment failures.

To do that, you must measure and chart the frequency of each incident. This way you can make individuals, teams, departments and organizations aware of failures to meet customer commitments and the costs of doing so.

Now the motivation exists not only to tackle the problems that really count but to allocate the resources necessary to solve them. Take, for example, the manager of a network of computer workstations who is specifically committed to provide computer support to a company's home office. With charted measurements, she can now recognize and *prove* that productivity drops severely whenever machines break down unexpectedly. Now she can move aggressively toward a solution and gain the support she needs to fix the problem.

BACK TO SYSTEM IMPROVEMENT

At this point, the process dovetails into the first step of the generalized manufacturing model in Figure 1. But now, instead of just "selecting a problem," you know *which* problem to select—the one that will yield the greatest return on investment.

Our computer network manager, for instance, can now use the traditional quality improvement steps just as a shop foreman would. The problem identified is unscheduled computer and workstation downtime. The current process is mapped. The cause is found. A solution—regular scheduled maintenance and replacement of computer components—is decided on. This solution is mapped, tested and documented, then implemented.

Note that during the data-gathering process every effort has gone into serving customers to the level of your written commitments. Customers have thus been retained because commitment failures have been remedied (for the most part) on the spot. Everyone in the company has been fully involved in the process, and they know the costs of poor service, whether internal or external. No resources have been diverted from serving the customers, and you avoided the intensive, highly specialized paperwork symptomatic of the traditional quality process. Plans have been advanced (based on hard data) to attack real—not imagined—system problems that pay off in terms of better customer support and satisfaction.

By following this four-step process, nonmanufacturing organization and departments can move ahead with quality improvement instead of getting bogged down in it. Good results begin to appear immediately, not two or more years down the road. This rapid-deployment process fits quality improvement with the rest of the daily work, without wasted effort on mapping the wrong problems. The process is not especially complicated, so it's easy to get going and to keep active throughout the organization. Economically speaking, it offers a good return on time and resources invested.

Genuine quality improvement—the kind that makes a difference to customers and builds a stronger, more competitive organization—really is achievable by people in nonmanufacturing jobs. This better, faster approach deserves the attention of any organization sincere about doing the best it can—which is the real quality imperative.

Gary K. Johnson is president of WMI Corp. of Bellevue, WA, a publisher of training programs. Roland A. Dumas, Ph.D. is president of Roberts Information Services of San Mateo, CA, and a judge for the Malcom Baldridge National Quality Awards.

Just what, exactly, is quality service?

"When I was a banker at a community bank in Indiana, I read that the largest banks were all trying to cut back on their waiting times," says J. Douglas Adamson, now executive director of the American Bankers Association and its Bank Marketing Association subsidiary. "So I decided that we had to work on cutting down our waiting time. As I started campaigning for shorter waiting times in the branches, I discovered that we had no waiting time."

This is one of many examples Adamson gives of off-target service quality programs. Another is the time he got a scratch on the hood of his new car and went to a body shop to have it fixed.

"The service people were very courteous," he remembers. "They gave me a ride back to the bank in a courtesy van and later gave me a ride back to the shop when the car was ready. When they brought the car out, it had been washed and looked beautiful except that the trunk had been painted a different color." The service people were very apologetic and gave him another ride in the courtesy van. The second time, the car was painted the right color, but it had a swirl pattern on it. The employees again were apologetic and pleasant, and after their third try the car was presentable.

That was a case of great customer relations but poor performance, Adamson relates. The bottom line he adds is that, "I will never go back there again."

Another anecdote involves a bank that redesigned its lobbies, only to find that its customers didn't care how the branches looked, but did care about whether or not their account statements had errors.

"Improving service quality is deciding what to change, whether it be an attitude, a behavior, a procedure, a policy, a product, a system, or a process," Adamson says. "Research helps reduce the risk of making a bad decision. If repapering the lobby will have a negligible affect on customers, why not spend that money elsewhere? Maybe

Commercial Banks Quality Focus Service Strategy Map

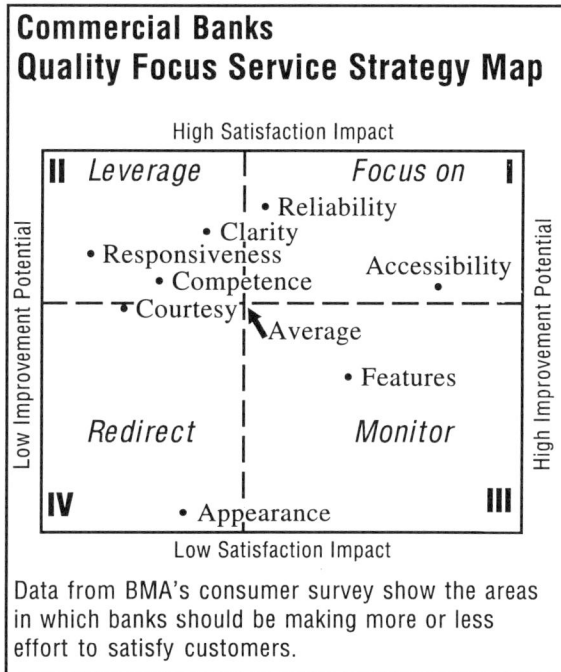

High Satisfaction Impact

II Leverage   Focus on I
                    • Reliability
              • Clarity
• Responsiveness   Accessibility
        • Competence   •
      • Courtesy
                  Average

                    • Features

    Redirect   Monitor

IV   • Appearance   III

Low Satisfaction Impact

Low Improvement Potential / High Improvement Potential

Data from BMA's consumer survey show the areas in which banks should be making more or less effort to satisfy customers.

you should be investing in Skylink [ABA's satellite-delivered training program] instead of skylights," he suggests.

BMA's Quality Focus Institute addressed this need for focused efforts with a national consumer survey it conducted earlier this year. It mailed a 72-question survey to 20,004 households and received 1,700 responses.

"The news is generally good, but there is room for improvement," Adamson says of the results of the *1992 National Consumer Study on Service Quality in Banking.*

Overall scores. First, people were asked about their overall satisfaction with their bank.

A little more than half (50.9%) of the respondents were highly satisfied, in other words they rated their bank a nine or a ten on a scale of one to ten. The average score was 8.13.

Overall satisfaction was lowest in New York, New Jersey, and Pennsylvania. New England states also faired poorly. Satisfaction was highest in Alabama, Kentucky, Mississippi, and Tennessee, closely followed by Illinois, Indiana, Michigan, Ohio, and Wisconsin.

Less than half (47.9%) would definitely recommend their bank to a friend or relative who had just moved to the area. Another 10.6% said they would not recommend their bank.

Affluent respondents were much less likely to recommend their bank than those with lower incomes, and people over the age of 65 were much more likely to recommend their bank than those under 35.

"Affluent people are more sophisticated, use more products, and demand a higher service level," explains Adamson. Older people, with more time to be satisfied, are more inclined to accept lower levels of service, he noted.

When asked if their satisfaction with their bank had changed within the last six months, 12.3% said they were less satisfied, 7.4% said they were more satisfied, and the other 80% reported no change.

Homing In. The crux of the survey, however, was the eight areas in which banks can most accurately measure their service quality, according to the Quality Focus Institute. These are: accessibility, appearance, clarity, competence, courtesy, features, reliability, and responsiveness. Survey respondents were asked about the importance they put on each of these items and how well their bank measured up.

Questions on *accessibility* covered hours and locations available, approachability of employees, and navigability of layout.

Appearance referred to the bank and its employees.

Clarity included communication of policies and terms.

Competence referred to employees' skill, knowledge, professionalism, and helpfulness.

Courtesy covered friendliness, considerateness, and respectfulness.

Features covered products, services, prices, and fees.

Reliability referred to consistent, accurate, and dependable delivery of products and services.

Responsiveness measured willingness to serve and quickness and correctness of answers to questions.

Overall, consumers felt that clarity, courtesy, and reliability were the most important areas. The respondents also said that those were the three areas where they were the most satisfied.

Deeper look. You could conclude from those two findings that banks are hitting the nail on the head when it comes to service.

But the overall numbers are not the whole story, according to BMA. The Quality Focus Institute further analyzed each consumer's responses in a series of calculations.

The calculations produced five service quality factors:

(1) "Service magnitude"—the value of perceived importance and satisfaction combined for each of the eight service attributes described above;

(2) "Service gap"—the degree to which each attribute offers opportunities for service quality improvement;

(3) "Maximum attainable satisfaction"—the standard against which each service quality area should be independently measured;

(4) "Improvement potential"—the amount of room for improvement; and

(5) "Satisfaction impact"—the statistical relationship between customers' overall satisfaction with financial institutions and their satisfaction with each of the eight service quality areas at their bank.

From these calculations, the Quality Focus Institute generated a series of "service strategy maps." These are charts with a vertical axis representing satisfaction impact and a horizontal axis representing improvement potential. The eight service quality areas are plotted in the four sections of the chart. Those attributes that appear in the quadrant where high improvement potential meets high satisfaction impact are the ones to be focused on.

The accompanying map shows the results for all commercial banks. It indicates that "reliability" and "accessibility" are most important to this broad cross-section of respondents. The maps for each region had a very different look, however. In most of the regions, "features," "responsiveness," and "competence" were the top areas. On the other hand, "accessibility" ranked higher than features in New Jersey, New York, Pennsylvania, Arkansas, Louisiana, Oklahoma, and Texas.

Local focus. Although the survey results and maps are important benchmarks, each bank and each neighborhood are different.

Thus, BMA offers a *Service Quality Satisfaction Analysis,* in which it will survey a bank's customers, make the five calculations described above, and produce charts and a strategy map.

The important thing is to strive for continuous quality improvement. "Banks need an Olympic gold medalist mindset: zero defects, zero defections," Adamson says. "Uptime of 98% on ATMs may sound good, but if you have 1,000 ATMs, that means you have 20 ATMs not working at any time, which is not that good."

AMERICA'S
Quality Coaches

By James Gagne

A look at their game plans for turning firms into winners

Quality, the cornerstone of competitive strategy for firms that hope to survive the 20th century, is having a profound effect on the way companies are managed. American business is being drawn into the quality revolution by the ever-growing expectations of customers around the world, who are demanding high quality products and services at low prices. For those that succeed, the evidence shows clearly that quality has become the key to increasing both market share and profits.

While some U.S. firms have turned to promotional gimmicks to improve their quality image, many are making dramatic changes and finding that a real commitment to meeting higher quality goals also results in higher

productivity, thereby lowering costs.

A small group of "quality experts" have been saying for years that quality is a cost effective and necessary business strategy. Today, a growing number of U.S. firms are following the coaching of these experts in an effort to compete. Four of the most sought after "quality coaches" are W. Edwards Deming, Joseph M. Juran, William E. Conway, and Philip B. Crosby.

All of them recognize that there are no short cuts to quality, and that the improvement process is a never-ending cycle, requiring the full support and participation of individual workers, whole departments, and, most importantly, top management.

Beyond that, the four coaches disagree about how best to go about improving quality. This report presents their individual "game plans" for American business.

Dr. W. Edwards Deming is the 85-year-old statistician best known for setting Japanese business upon the course that has made them number one in quality throughout the world. In 1950, he went to Japan to help the U.S. Secretary of War conduct a population census, and was invited to lecture to top business leaders on statistical quality control. Deming told the Japanese they could "take over the world" if they followed his advice. The rest is history, and today the highest quality award in Japan is named after Deming. He has been called the "founder of the Third Wave of the Industrial Revolution," and often sounds like a crusader for quality with statements such as, "it is time to adopt a new religion in America."

He estimates that it will take the United States 30 years to accomplish what the Japanese have done to improve quality because "a big ship, traveling at full speed, requires distance and time to turn." He warns that "people who expect quick results are doomed to disappointment."

According to Deming, good quality does not necessarily mean high quality. It is, rather, "a predictable degree of uniformity and dependability, at low cost, and suited to the market." He recognizes that the quality of any product or service has many scales, and may get a high mark on one scale and a low mark on another. In other words, quality is whatever the customer needs and wants. And since the customer's requirements and tastes are always changing, the solution to defining quality in terms of the customer is to constantly conduct customer research.

Deming's basic philosophy on quality is that productivity improves as variability decreases. Since all things vary, he says, that is why the

Deming claims that management is responsible for 94 percent of quality problems, and points out that it is management's task to help people work smarter, not harder.

statistical method of quality control is needed. "Statistical control does not imply absence of defective items. It is a state of random variation, in which the limits of variation are predictable," he explains.

There are two types of variation: chance and assignable, and says Deming, "The difference between these is one of the most difficult things to comprehend." It is a waste of time and money to look for the cause of chance variation, yet, he says, this is exactly what many companies do when they attempt to solve quality problems without using statistical methods. He advocates the use of statistics to measure performance in all areas, not just conformance to product specifications. Furthermore, he says it is not enough to meet specifications; one has to keep working to reduce the variation as well.

Deming is extremely critical of U.S. management and is an advocate of worker participation in decision making. He claims that management is responsible for 94 percent of quality problems, and points out that it is management's task to help people work smarter, not harder. "The first step is for management to remove the barriers that rob the hourly worker of his right to do a good job," he says.

He also knocks motivational programs, in which he includes zero defects, and says that everyone simply doing their best is not the answer because it is also necessary that people know what to do. And, he asks, "How can a man do it right the first time when the incoming material is off gauge, off color, or otherwise defective, or if his machine is not in good order?"

Deming cites the following as a typical letter from a supplier in response to an inquiry on its quality: "We are pleased to inform you that quality is our motto. We believe in quality. You will see from the enclosed pamphlet that nothing goes out of this plant until it has been thoroughly inspected. In fact, a large portion of our effort in production is spent in inspection to be sure of our quality." This, he says, "is a true confession of ignorance of what quality is, and how to achieve it."

Inspection, whether of incoming or outgoing goods, is, according to Deming, too late, ineffective, and costly. "Inspection does not improve quality, nor guarantee it," he says. Moreover, inspection is usually designed to allow a

certain number of defects to enter the system. For example, a company that buys items with an acceptable quality level of three percent is, in effect, telling the vendor that it can send three bad items out of every 100. "The vendor will be pleased to meet these requirements," says Deming.

He says that judging quality requires knowledge of the "statistical evidence of quality," and that companies dealing with vendors under statistical control can eliminate inspection. "You will note from the control charts that came along with the product, far better than any inspection can tell you, what the distribution of quality is, and what it will be tomorrow." In this way, quality is predictable, and one can also safely predict that the vendor's quality will improve over time. "One of the first steps for managers of purchasing to take is to learn enough about the statistical control of quality to be able to assess the qualifications of a supplier, to be able to talk to him in statistical language," says Deming.

Deming also points out that simply checking the specifications of incoming materials may not be enough if the material encounters problems in production. "Specifications cannot tell the

whole story. The supplier must know what the material is to be used for," he says.

He is critical of most procedures for qualifying vendors on quality because once qualified, the vendor "has discharged his responsibility, and the purchaser accepts whatever he gets." The only effective way to qualify vendors is to see if their management abides by his 14 points, uses statistical process control, and is willing to cooperate on tests and use of instructions and gauges.

The best recognition one can give a quality vendor, according to Deming, is to give that vendor more business. He points out that requiring statistical evidence of process control in selecting vendors would mean, in most companies, a drastic reduction in the number of vendors they deal with simply because not that many vendors would qualify. Nevertheless, he says, this is the only way to choose vendors, even if that means relying on a single source for critical items. In fact, Deming advocates single sourcing. "A second source, for protection, for every item purchased is a costly practice," he says. The advantages of single sourcing include better vendor commitment, eliminating small differences between products from two suppliers, and simplifying accounting and paperwork.

As to the fact that relying on a single source can often mean paying a higher price, Deming says, "The policy of forever trying to drive down the price of anything purchased, with no regard to quality and service, can drive good vendors and good service out of business. The ways of doing business with

"People who expect quick results are doomed to disappointment."

W. Edwards Deming

vendors and customers that were good enough in the past must now be revised to meet new requirements of quality and productivity."

Deming works as a private consultant to dozens of firms in the United States. It is said that he will simply stop working with a client who does not show a total commitment to quality.

Deming's 14 Points for Management

1. Create constancy of purpose toward improvement of product and service.

2. Adopt the new philosophy. We can no longer live with commonly accepted levels of delays, mistakes, defective materials, and defective workmanship.

3. Cease dependence on mass inspection. Require, instead, statistical evidence that quality is built in.

4. End the practice of awarding business on the basis of price tag.

5. Find problems. It is management's job to work continually on the system.

6. Institute modern methods of training on the job.

7. Institute modern methods of supervision of production workers. The responsibility of foremen must be changed from numbers to quality.

8. Drive out fear, so that everyone may work effectively for the company.

9. Break down barriers between departments.

10. Eliminate numerical goals, posters, and slogans for the work force, asking for new levels of productivity without providing methods.

11. Eliminate work standards that prescribe numerical quotas.

12. Remove barriers that stand between the hourly worker and his right to pride of workmanship.

13. Institute a vigorous program of education and retraining.

14. Create a structure in top management that will push every day on the above 13 points.

Joseph M. Juran was born 81 years ago in Rumania, and came to the United States in 1912. After studying electrical engineering and law, he rose to chief of the inspection control division of Western Electric Co. and professor at New York University. Juran, like Deming, is credited with part of the quality success story of Japan, where he went in 1954 to lecture on how to manage for quality. He is the author of numerous books on quality and management, as well as editor of the "Quality Control Handbook." In 1979, he founded the Juran Institute, which conducts quality training seminars.

According to Juran, there are two kinds of quality: "fitness for use" and "conformance to specifications." To illustrate the difference, he says a dangerous product could meet all specifications, but not be fit for use.

Juran was the first to deal with the broad management aspects of quality, which distinguishes him from those who espouse specific techniques, statistical or otherwise. In the 1940s, he pointed out that the technical aspects of quality control had been well covered, but that firms did not know how to manage for quality. He identified some of the problems as organization, communication, and coordination of functions—in other words, the human element. According to Juran, "An understanding of the human situations associated with the job will go far to solve the technical problems; in fact such understanding may be a prerequisite of a solution." For example, an inspector may incorrectly interpret the specifications and thus subvert quality control efforts, or worse, he may knowingly protect favored operators or suppliers.

Juran talks about three basic steps to progress: structured annual improvements combined with devotion and a sense of urgency, massive training programs, and upper management leadership. In his view less that 20% of quality problems are due to workers, with the remainder being caused by management. Just as all managers need some training in finance, all should have training in quality in order to oversee and participate in quality improvement projects. And *top* management should be included because, "all major quality problems are interdepartmental." Moreover, pursuing departmental goals can sometimes undermine a company's overall quality mission, he says.

Companies should avoid "campaigns to motivate the

In the 1940s, Juran pointed out that the technical aspects of quality control had been well covered, but that firms did not know how to manage for quality.

workforce to solve the company's quality problems by doing perfect work," says Juran, because these "exhortation-only" approaches and slogans "fail to set specific goals, establish specific plans to meet these goals, or provide the needed resources." He notes, however, that upper managers like these programs because they do not detract from their time.

Juran favors the concept of quality circles because they improve communications between management and labor. He also recommends using statistical process control, but warns that it can lead to a "tool-oriented" approach. Juran does not believe that "quality is free." He explains

that because of the law of diminishing returns, there is an optimum point of quality, beyond which conformance is more costly than the value of the quality obtained.

He recognizes purchasing's important role in quality improvement. "A company cannot produce greater precision in *vacuo*; it must secure greater precision from its suppliers." Juran also recognizes that purchasing's task can be much more complex than ordinarily assumed. For example, he addresses the problems of assessing the quality of contractors competing for big one-of-a-kind projects, as well as how to deal with unexpected changes in specifications.

Typical of his penchant for looking at the "big picture," Juran points out that the same time that buyers are recognizing the need for better communications with suppliers, more and more of these suppliers are foreign firms. This puts up potential barriers to communications due to language and other cultural differences. He also points to different technological standards throughout the world and the fact that international standardization is lengthy and slow.

Juran is not in favor of single sourcing for important purchases, which he defines as product-related items such as raw materials or components. "For important purchases it is well to use multiple sources of supply. A single source can more easily neglect to sharpen its competitive edge in quality, cost, and service," he says.

Training for purchasing managers should include techniques for rating vendors, according to Juran, and he adds that rating vendors is only half of the process. The customer must also "make the investment of time, effort and special skills to help the poor vendors improve."

To qualify vendors on quality, purchasing needs to do a formal survey to insure

Juran's 10 Steps to Quality Improvement

1. Build awareness of the need and opportunity for improvement.

2. Set goals for improvement.

3. Organize to reach the goals (establish a quality council, identify problems, select projects, appoint teams, designate facilitators).

4. Provide training.

5. Carry out projects to solve problems.

6. Report progress.

7. Give recognition.

8. Communicate results.

9. Keep score.

10. Maintain momentum by making annual improvement part of the regular systems and processes of the company.

A company cannot produce greater precision in vacuo; it must secure greater precision from its suppliers.

Joseph M. Juran

that the vendor can consistently manufacture to specifications. Comparing U.S. and Japanese vendor qualifying practices, Juran says those in the United States are not as effective. "To predict vendor adequacy, U.S. firms studied the suppliers' systems—organization, written procedures, manuals, audits and so on. The Japanese firms looked at process capabilities, process controls, acceptance of teamwork relationships, extent of quality control training, and quality of prior deliveries." He is critical of arm's-length and adversary relationships with vendors, and says they should be part of the team.

The Juran Institute teaches a project-by-project, problem-solving, team method of quality improvement, in which upper management must be involved. "The project approach is important. When it comes to quality, there is no such thing as improvement in general. Any improvement in quality is going to come about project by project and no other way," says Juran.

Philip B. Crosby is the 59-year-old quality expert best known for coming up with the concept of zero defects in the early 1960s when he was in charge of quality for the Pershing missile project at Martin Corp. In 1965, he went to ITT as director of quality, and left in 1979 to form Philip Crosby Associates. He got into consulting and writing because "I was tired of hearing how the United States was going down the chute." His book, *Quality Is Free,* has sold more than one million copies.

According to Crosby's definition, quality is conformance to requirements, and it can only be measured by the cost of nonconformance. "Don't talk about poor quality or high quality. Talk about conformance and nonconformance," he says. This approach means that the only standard of performance is zero defects.

If he had to sum up in a single word what quality management is all about, Crosby says the word would be "prevention." Whereas the conventional view says quality is achieved through inspection, testing, and checking, he says that prevention is the only system that can be utilized. And when Crosby says "prevention" he means "perfection." There is no

Whereas the conventional view says quality is achieved through inspection, testing, and checking, Crosby says that prevention is the only system that can be utilized.

place in his philosophy for statistically acceptable levels of quality. "People go to great elaborate things to develop statistical levels of compliance. We've learned to believe that error is inevitable, and to plan for it." But, he says, "There is absolutely no reason for having errors or defects in any product."

Crosby talks about a quality "vaccine" that firms can use to prevent nonconformances. The three ingredients of this vaccine are determination, education, and implementation. He points out that quality improvement is a process not a program, saying, "Nothing permanent or lasting ever comes from a program."

He says quality is management's responsibility, and that "We have to be as concerned about quality as we are about profit." He is doubtful, however, that this change in attitude will occur in this generation because most companies continue to compound quality problems by "hassling" their employees, which renders them demotivated by the "thoughtless, irritating, unconcerned way they are dealt with." Crosby says a committed management can obtain a 40 percent reduction in error rates very quickly from a committed workforce, while eliminating the remaining error takes a little more work.

One misconception concerning Crosby is that he is primarily advocating prodding workers into performing better. He explains the root of this misconception, saying,

Crosby's 14 Steps to Quality Improvement

1. Make it clear that management is committed to quality.

2. Form quality improvement teams with representatives from each department.

3. Determine where current and potential quality problems lie.

4. Evaluate the cost of quality and explain its use as a management tool.

5. Raise the quality awareness and personal concern of all employees.

6. Take action to correct problems identified through previous steps.

7. Establish a committee for the zero defects program.

8. Train supervisors to actively carry out their part of the quality improvement program.

9. Hold a 'zero defects day' to let all employees realize that there has been a change.

10. Encourage individuals to establish improvement goals for themselves and their groups.

11. Encourage employees to communicate to management the obstacles they face in attaining their improvement goals.

12. Recognize and appreciate those who participate.

13. Establish quality councils to communicate on a regular basis.

14. Do it all over again to emphasize that the quality improvement program never ends.

We have to be as concerned about quality as we are about profit.

Philip B. Crosby

"Unfortunately, zero defects was picked up by industry as a 'motivation' program." In 1964, the Japanese adopted zero defects, and Crosby says they were the only ones who correctly applied it—as a management performance standard rather than a motivation program for employees.

Crosby says that in purchased items, at least half of quality problems are caused by not clearly stating what the requirements are. Since defects are defined as deviations from the published, announced, or agreed-upon requirements, a lot of effort and thought should go into those requirements. In this, he points to the example of Japan, where "they treat the supplier as an extension of their own business."

As it is now, he says, "Half of the rejections that occur are the fault of the purchaser." For this reason, Crosby recommends rating buyers as well as vendors. "In tracking purchasing agents you find that they have a built in defect rate," he explains.

Visiting a potential supplier to conduct a quality audit is next to useless, according to Crosby. "Unless the vendor is a complete and obvious disaster area, it is impossible to know whether their quality system will provide the proper control or not."

Philip Crosby Associates offers company-wide training through its Quality College, and is now expanding from management training to supplying training materials and training instructors.

William E. Conway is a relative newcomer to the quality game. Born 60 years ago, he graduated from Harvard and the U.S. Naval Academy before beginning a business career that would lead him to the top as president and chairman of Nashua Corp. In 1979, he invited Dr. Deming to Nashua Corp. to help improve the firm's quality. The visit lasted three years, and in 1983, he founded Conway Quality, Inc. Because of his close association with Deming, he is sometimes described as a "Deming disciple," but Conway has

Conway says it is possible to continually improve the productivity and quality performance of everyone in a firm on a monthly basis.

developed his own plan for quality improvement.

He does not talk in terms of a specific definition of quality per se. Instead, he incorporates that into his broad definition of quality management, which he says is "development, manufacture, administration, and distribution of consistent low cost products and services that customers want and/or need." Quality management also means constant improvement in all areas of operations, including suppliers and distributors, to eliminate waste of material, capital, and time. The wasting of time is, by far, the biggest waste that occurs in most organizations, according to Conway. Excess inventory is another important form of waste because, he says, 60 percent of the space commonly used is not needed, yet a company must pay for it, pay to maintain it, and pay taxes on it.

Taking the view of the man who has been there at the top of a corporation, Conway talks about the "right way to manage" rather than simply how to improve quality. He says the biggest problem is that top management is not convinced that quality increases productivity and lowers costs. Furthermore, they feel they don't have time to

deal with the problem. "The bottleneck is located at the top of the bottle."

What is required is the creation of a new "system of management," whose primary task is continuous improvement in all areas. This, he says, is the most important change, and means changing all the unwritten rules in a company, and giving people positive reinforcement. "People work *in* the system, management works *on* the system. Workers will welcome the change," promises Conway. And while critical of U.S. management, he recognizes that "management wants and needs real help—not destructive criticism."

Conway is a strong advocate of using statistical methods to achieve quality gains, and says that one of the greatest handicaps lies in attempting to deal with productivity and quality in generalities. "The use of statistics is a common sense way of getting into specifics," he says, adding, "Statistics don't solve problems. They identify where the problems are and point managers and workers toward solutions."

He distinguishes between simple and sophisticated statistical techniques, which he calls "tools." The simple

statistical tools are run charts, flow charts, fishbone charts, Pareto charts, histograms, and correlations charts. Surveys of customers are one of the most important tools because they tell a firm what to work on. According to Conway, these simple techniques can be used to solve 85 percent of a company's problems, while more complicated statistical process control methods are needed only about 15 percent of the time.

Furthermore, Conway points out that once a process is in control, the people responsible for it become more creative in eliminating variations because they know that they are personally capable of improving the system. In fact, people at the bottom make the most improvement because they learn "how to be logical all the time." Conway says this also applies to R & D operations, and since the United States is still the world leader in creativity and innovation, he is optimistic about its future.

Conway says it is possible to continually improve the productivity and quality performance of everyone in a firm on a monthly basis. "In less than one year, you ought to be able to perform miracles," he predicts. This miracle has already been performed by the Japanese, who have caused what Conway terms a "paradigm shift" in the way the world views quality. This shift is comparable to the discovery, centuries ago, that the earth was round.

In his talks, Conway does not dwell for long on purchasing or any other function because he believes his principles apply to all areas. Focusing efforts on one area is not sufficient to change the management "system" of a company. He says, however, that the creation and implementation of the new system is intended to be customized for each department. In fact, it is not necessary to wait for someone at the top to start

Statistics don't solve problems. They identify where the problems are and point managers and workers towards solutions.

William E. Conway

the change; they can be shown by example the "right way to manage."

Conway's call for constant improvement in all areas of operations is intended to include a company's suppliers, and here, too, the key to success is the use of statistics. "It is just as vital to achieve statistical control of quality from your vendors as it is to have it internally," he says.

Overspecification, another form of waste in Conway's view, is not solely the responsibility of engineers. Purchasing managers and anyone connected with the design of a product are also responsible. He warns that specifications—like work standards—sometimes "cap" improvements.

In addition to working closely with clients, Conway Quality also provides training materials and furnishes a three-month implementation plan for management, called the "Gold Plan," which is a step-by-step plan for improving quality and productivity.

Conway's 6 Tools for Quality Improvement.

1. Human relations skills—the responsibility of management to create at every level, among all employees, the motivation and training to make the necessary improvements in the organization.

2. Statistical surveys—the gathering of data about customers (internal as well as external), employees, technology and equipment, to be used as a measure for future progress and to identify what needs to be done.

3. Simple statistical techniques—clear charts and diagrams that help identify problems, track work flow, gauge progress, and indicate solutions.

4. Statistical process control—the statistical charting of a process, whether manufacturing or non-manufacturing, to help identify and reduce variation.

5. Imagineering—a key concept in problem solving, involves the visualization of a process, procedure, or operation with all waste eliminated.

6. Industrial engineering—common techniques of pacing, work simplification, methods analysis, plant layout and material handling to achieve improvements.

Special Report

CUS FOCUSING ON QUALITY

TOTAL QUALITY MANAGEMENT (TQM) is playing a prominent role in large credit union's strategic plans, according to a survey of 500 large credit unions. *Ninety-three percent of respondents say TQM is an extremely or somewhat important issue for credit unions* during the next three to five years (Figure 1).

The reason behind TQM's sudden prominence is "members are becoming more sensitive to the quality of financial services," says Mike Miller, manager of Business Development Services for CUNA Mutual Insurance Group, Madison, Wis., and a member of the National Credit Union Quality Network. The network—comprised primarily of senior management staff from eight credit unions—conducted the survey.

More credit unions are turning to TQM as a way to stay competitive in an increasingly quality-focused market. *Nearly two-thirds of credit unions in the study (62%) already have TQM programs in place.* Twenty-four percent of credit unions with TQM programs have had their programs in place for less than one year.

A formal TQM definition is hard to come by because there are many variations on the central TQM theme. There are many TQM proponents, and each takes a slightly different approach to achieving quality.

Members' needs are at the core of credit union TQM programs. Your members are judge and jury when it comes to the quality of your credit union's services. *TQM recognizes that 85% of an organization's problems have to do with processes—not individuals.* TQM gives process

Figure 1. **How Important Is TQM to Your Credit Union's Future?**

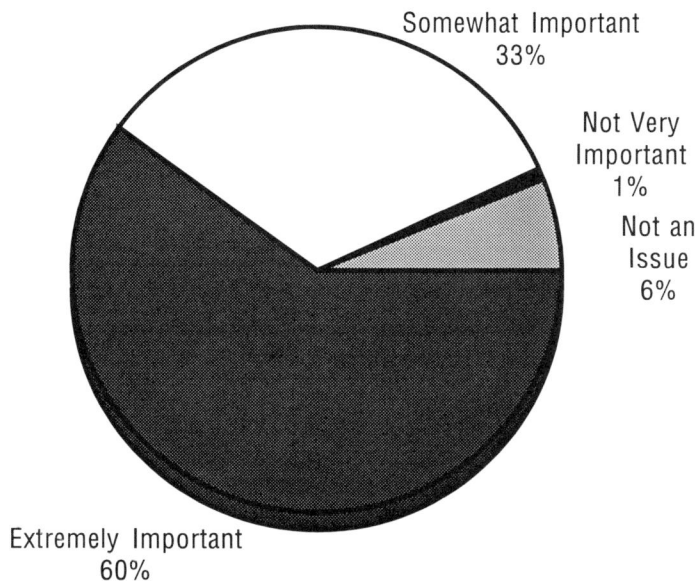

Somewhat Important
33%

Not Very
Important
1%

Not an
Issue
6%

Extremely Important
60%

Source: National Credit Union Quality Network. Reprinted by permission.

owners (employees) power to improve the process; recognizes the value and necessity of teamwork and partnerships; requires that decisions be based on data, not supposition; and uses scientific research to collect data.

But no two TQM programs are alike. "One credit union's quality environment will be completely different from that of another," says Miller. "And even within the same organization, it's common to have multiple definitions of quality."

There are, however, some common characteristics. *Credit unions in the study list four of them crucial to a TQM program's success:*

1. *Training and education.* The primary element of success is instructing all staff about TQM philosophy, principles, and practices.

University of Wisconsin Credit Union, Madison, Wis., opens late on Wednesday mornings so employees can attend a quality training program called Team Teach. Employees also attend graduate-level TQM classes at the university's School of Business. "Everyone in the credit union, from the president on down, receives quality im-

provement training," says Dave Baggett, the credit union's vice president of business development and planning.

2. *An environment in which employees have authority to make changes.* Sixty-two percent of credit unions in the survey say their employees have authority to make quality improvements to their own jobs. "Our employees welcome the responsibility of taking care of our systems and our basic operational quality," says Baggett. "They understand what's expected of them, and we're introducing them to the tools they'll use to achieve that quality."

*Nearly all credit unions (95%) that give employees authority to make quality improvements use training and education to explain the process...*95% use directives from senior management...50% employ performance standards...38% use incentives and promotions.

The process of giving employees this authority removes many traditional communication barriers. Digital Employees Federal Credit Union, Maynard,

Mass., began its quality program earlier this year. "Several employees say things really are changing, and the barriers are coming down between employees and management," says Karen Wall, Digital Employees' director of human resources.

3. *Results measurement.* Measuring your results helps justify your work and determine where you can continue to improve.

In addition to assessing increased earnings and faster turnaround times, some credit unions are benchmarking their results (comparing them with those of similar organizations). North Island Federal Credit Union, Chula Vista, Calif., compares its results with other financial institutions and with other service companies. Mike Maslak, North Island Federal's chief executive officer (CEO), is a national quality examiner who helps determine Baldridge Award winners. The Baldridge Award is the government's award for quality in U.S. organizations.

4. *Commitment from the top.* TQM, like other popular management techniques, receives its share of skepticism for being "the flavor of the month." Skeptics recall

too many ill-fated management programs like management by objective, systematic performance awards and recognition— programs that were long on glitter but short on management follow-through. For a TQM program to be successful, employees must be convinced that the program has total and long-term commitment from top management. "We work hard to let employees know TQM is not just a fad at our credit union," says Wall.

It might take three to five years for TQM results to be fully realized. Management needs to resist the temptation to dump TQM when results

aren't immediate. "Total quality is a journey, never a destination," says Maslak.

Quality practices help your credit union improve operations and member service. While many think of TQM in relation to manufacturing, quality has applications in a service environment, too.

"If any group is best suited for TQM, it's credit unions," says Geri Dillingham, North Island Federal's senior vice president of marketing. "Credit unions have excelled in service management for years. TQM is a logical next step."

TQM is working well at North Island Federal. "We have a 97% member-satisfaction rating," says Dillingham. "The national average, ac-

cording to the American Bankers Association, is 70% to 80%."

TQM techniques have reduced North Island Federal's employee turnover rate from 38% in 1990, to 25% in 1991, and to 16% in 1992. The credit union also credits TQM for doubling its reserves in the past five years.

Most credit unions probably haven't seen these kinds of results—yet. North Island Federal is in the sixth year of its TQM program, while most credit unions are new to TQM. Only 15% of credit unions in the survey have been involved with TQM for three years or more, and half of the respondents classify themselves as TQM beginners.

Table 1. **Seven-Step Improvement Process**

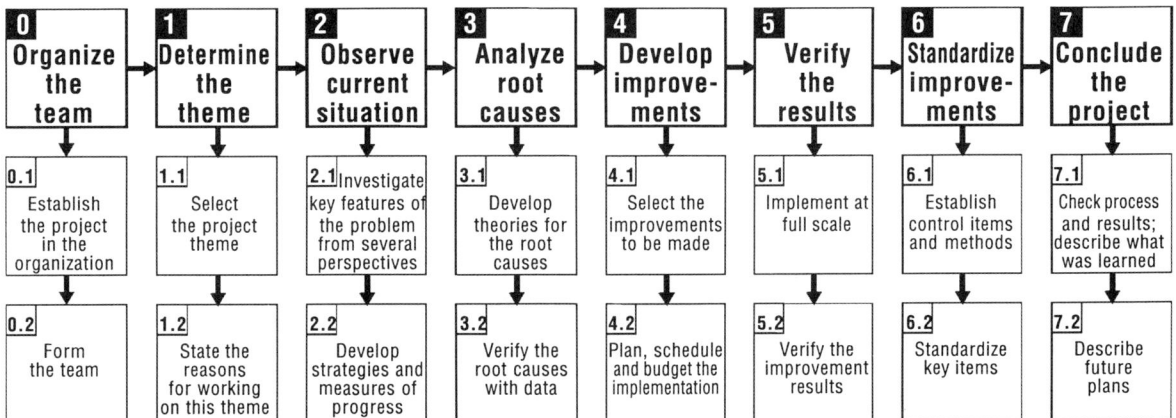

0 Organize the team	**1** Determine the theme	**2** Observe current situation	**3** Analyze root causes	**4** Develop improvements	**5** Verify the results	**6** Standardize improvements	**7** Conclude the project
0.1 Establish the project in the organization	**1.1** Select the project theme	**2.1** Investigate key features of the problem from several perspectives	**3.1** Develop theories for the root causes	**4.1** Select the improvements to be made	**5.1** Implement at full scale	**6.1** Establish control items and methods	**7.1** Check process and results; describe what was learned
0.2 Form the team	**1.2** State the reasons for working on this theme	**2.2** Develop strategies and measures of progress	**3.2** Verify the root causes with data	**4.2** Plan, schedule and budget the implementation	**5.2** Verify the improvement results	**6.2** Standardize key items	**7.2** Describe future plans

"Seven-step Quality Improvement Process" by Mark P. Finster.

TQM programs, however, haven't worked for all credit unions, says Miller. "Some credit union CEOs have been disappointed in the results," he says. *Credit unions run into trouble when they pursue quality without first defining their goals.* It's possible to spend a lot of time improving processes that have little effect on member satisfaction or on your bottom line.

Another reason for failure is giving up too quickly. The TQM program at University of Wisconsin Credit Union is less than a year old, and patience is key, says Baggett. "Watching TQM is like watching a tree grow. If you sit around and watch it, you're not going to see any progress. But if you come back and check every once in a while, you'll be surprised how much growth there is." Most TQM gurus say it takes six to 10 years to have a fully mature quality environment.

There are a number of other stumbling blocks on the road to TQM success. Survey respondents list the following as *the most common barriers to achieving quality in their credit unions:*

■ No time to implement a quality program. When daily operational duties call, it's hard to find time for training and team projects. Employees already are stretched to their limits. The irony, says Miller, is that *properly implemented TQM practices improve processes—and save time.*

■ Employees don't understand what TQM is trying to accomplish. Nearly three in five credit unions surveyed (58%) say their employees have *limited understanding of TQM.* It can be difficult gathering enough information to start a TQM program. Ask your league or other credit unions about proven TQM techniques.

■ Luke-warm commitment from credit union management. TQM requires a rethinking of the managing process—nearly half of the credit unions surveyed (46%) have changed their management structure to better achieve their quality goals. Some credit unions, however, found *management unwilling to let go of traditional decision-making processes.*

■ Quality improvement can be hard to measure. Some credit unions have trouble defining quality—only one in five have written quality standards. When you don't know how to define quality, measuring it becomes nearly impossible.

Here are three tips for starting a quality program:

1. Customize the program to your credit union. There's no TQM blueprint or rigid set of rules to follow. Seek out expert advice. And remember, there's more than one way to achieve your desired results.

2. Start small. Organizations that jump headfirst into quality management often drown. There are many no or low-cost ways to recognize and reward employees, and to promote a service atmosphere, says Dillingham. She suggests starting on a small scale, with strong commitment from top management.

3. Do your own benchmarking. "There's a lot of interest in the National Credit Union Quality Network," says Miller. "Sharing information and benchmarks prevents credit unions from duplicating mistakes." For more information about the quality network, contact Jane Ronnfeldt, vice president of marketing, San Bernardino (Calif.) County Central Credit Union; (714) 881-3355.

How to Get Your TQM Training on Track

By Patricia A. Galagan

For small and midsize businesses, just figuring out how to learn the skills of quality management can be a daunting task.

Of the 20 million small businesses in the U.S., only a handful are practicing true Total Quality Management. A few more are somewhere on the steep learning curve that gets companies to the point that they're ready for TQM.

For the rest, it's business as usual.

The pioneers have discovered that it takes training, training, and more training to be a quality company. Not just formal training in a classroom, but a whole range of learning experiences, from reading books to inventing new work processes as a team.

A common belief among companies just starting to pursue quality is that it can be learned quickly. The basic principles—focus on the customer, and continuously improve your product or service—seem simple enough. Until, that is, you start trying to apply them.

"You read about the need to be patient, and after a year of trying, I can say it's true," acknowledges Charles Jett Jr., of Premix Industries, a maker of just-add-water bagged concrete. The company, based in Chesapeake, Va., has 165 employees.

"Quality takes a long time to learn, and I wish we had accepted that earlier," Jett says. "It would have saved us a lot of anxiety and frustration. TQM turned out to be a much more encompassing philosophy than we thought. We thought we'd read a Deming book [management consultant W. Edwards Deming is a TQM pioneer] and maybe a book on teamwork and be done."

Lengthy preparation for the real action is common in small and midsize companies. People spend what seem like huge amounts of time reading about quality or going to training courses, only to realize they don't know much and their company hasn't really started quality management.

"The TQM journey has a lot of surprises in it," says Pat Lancaster, president of Lantech, a manufacturing company of 330 employees in Louisville, Ky. Lantech makes machines that wrap large items in plastic.

"One of the surprises is the length of time it takes to actually begin," he says. "In our case it took two years."

Elaine Biech, a partner in "ebb associates" of Portage, Wis., has been a TQM consultant and trainer for several years. "The biggest problem we have is to put reins on people," she says. "They want to train everybody at once because training has been touted as the answer to all their quality problems." But the critical first step, she says, is to train the managers and supervisors thoroughly, "so that when the rest of the staff comes out of training they won't get shut down for practicing their new skills."

Building a friendly environment for TQM—what quality consultants call a culture—is some of the hardest work they've ever done, say people who've been through it.

"I was surprised at the degree of organizational shock we had to go through," Pat Lancaster recalls. The top managers in his family-owned business had to make a commitment to change some of the deeply held views about how to run things. Wrenching as that was, it was only the first step.

"An organization that has a belief in TQM and a commitment to it is only about 10 percent of the way there," Lancaster warns. "The key is to change behaviors and overcome resistance to those changes."

But what kind of training is most likely to bring about such change? You can choose among hundreds of versions of TQM. Whether sold by a single consultant or by a large training organization, each program reflects the values and beliefs of its inventor.

Most TQM training should cover some or all of a basic set of skills, says Richard Wellins, senior vice president of Design Dimensions International, of Pittsburgh. DDI is one of the biggest TQM vendors, with annual sales of $60 million. Those skills, he says, fall into three areas:

Leadership skills. These skills must be acquired by managers and supervisors. They must change their leadership behavior to become more receptive to ideas from others, to be coaches rather than controllers of people, and to facilitate things rather than mandate them.

Teamwork skills. TQM often involves working in teams. "Most people won't necessarily have the skills to work in teams as leaders or participants," Wellins says.

Technical skills. Sometimes called quality tools, these include dozens of methods for studying a problem

and displaying the results of analysis.

"A big mistake that companies can make about TQM training is to put people into classes without first figuring out what skills they need," warns Richard Chang, of Richard Chang and Associates, Inc., a consulting firm in Irvine, Calif. "Not everyone will need the same skills. It will depend on what business processes they work on, and who their customers are."

Many people in search of a TQM consultant or training program feel that they are about to swim in shark-infested waters. After several years of seeking help, Pat Lancaster warns: "There is bad information out there and a fair number of consultants who don't have the backbone to belly up to the client's table and get straight."

Premix Industries' Charlie Jett started by looking in the Yellow Pages under "Consultants." He says, "We interviewed them all and didn't like any of them." The local chamber of commerce directed him to the Total Quality Institute in Portsmouth, Va. It provided the course in group facilitation that Jett wanted.

Jim Zawacki, owner and president of Grand Rapids Spring & Wire Products, in Grand Rapids, Mich., with 160 employees, put his early money and training effort into "getting people to understand why we're in business" and into building "trust, relationships, integrity, and communications." He had no formal guide or mentor for this, only his own beliefs about quality management.

"I really believe that TQM starts with culture," he says, "and culture is the responsibility of management. It's taken years, but today we share financial statements with our people. They know that when we talk about improving an operation from a quality standpoint, we're not trying to eliminate jobs."

Zawacki says he also spent "a lot of money" on formal technical training, starting with statistical process control (SPC). Before these courses could begin, some employees needed to learn basic math skills. Zawacki taught those skills himself. For the SPC courses, he hired community college teachers.

A high level of care for employees and a big investment in training paid off for Grand Rapids Spring & Wire, Zawacki believes. In the past

five years, on-time delivery has gone from 60 percent to over 95 percent. Inventory has gone down 30 percent, and sales have doubled.

Lantech, the stretch-wrap machine manufacturer, bought mainly big-brand name consulting and training for its TQM effort. Like Zawacki, Lantech's president, Pat Lancaster, spent a lot of time—a year in his case—building commitment to the idea of TQM before buying training. To do this, teams of employees, including Lancaster, held many discussions about the human value in the company's vision and strategy.

Lancaster says he got his ideas about how to proceed "from the TQM salad bar of books and theories. Then he hired a business consulting firm to assess the levels of quality awareness of Lantech's top managers, middle managers, and people on the shop floor.

"They gave us a rather grim report," he recalls. "We hired them to help us along and we started some projects that were probably too large and grandiose."

A year later, Lantech hired a second consulting firm to assess its position again.

"They reported we were pretty close to where we were the first time," Lancaster admits. At that point, Lantech decided to do some in-house training because, he says, "we couldn't find training about quality that was consistent with our values."

From the president of another company Lancaster learned about the training firm Design Dimensions International. "We had a value alignment with DDI," he says. "They believed, as we did, that self-esteem boosts productivity, and that it's leadership's job to enhance self-esteem. We made an enormous investment in training, thousands of hours of training for over 300 employees."

Lantech now works with another large consulting company, Time-Based Management. Lancaster describes it as "a sort of graduate school for us." Time-Based Management provides technical training and has helped Lantech's engineering and manufacturing operations pick up their pace by encouraging employee teams to focus less on how they made decisions and more on how they carried them out.

After five years of effort and a major investment in

training, TQM seems to be working at Lantech. In a typical change, a process-improvement team, made up of floor workers, managers, and engineers, redesigned the process for building semi-automatic stretch-wrapping machines. Instead of building 10 machines at a time, as before, they now produce machines as customers order them.

Very few small companies can afford to buy TQM training directly from big-name vendors, as Lantech did; they must be more inventive in seeking help with TQM. But the motivation behind their search should be the same as the motivation behind Pat Lancaster's: to seek out the avenue to TQM that best fits their companies' values and circumstances.

The small company that approaches TQM in that spirit will find that it has plenty of options, even when its training budget is lean. Among them:

Hire small or midsize consulting firms. With lower overhead than the giants, they often can offer more-attractive deals.

Buy off-the-shelf training programs. Such training programs cost less than programs designed for specific customers. A middle-range option is to buy a packaged program from a supplier who can adapt it for your company, for a fee.

Form partnerships with local educational institutions. One way to enjoy the expertise of big-company consultants at small-company prices is to search out community colleges and vocational schools that will form training partnerships with small businesses. The schools license training from major training suppliers to avoid the costly and time-consuming task of developing training programs themselves. Zenger-Miller, an international training and consulting firm based in San Jose, Calif., has been taking part in such partnerships since 1983 and now serves schools in 23 states.

In any case, what is absolutely critical is not choosing a particular path to TQM, but making the unqualified commitment to find the path that is right for you. Lantech, for example, was able to keep pressing toward TQM, despite all its false starts and disappointments, because its owners and managers knew what they wanted to achieve.

"We didn't have the Japanese coming over the ocean and cleaning our clock," Pat Lancaster says. "No customer or competitor was pushing us. But there was something out of sync about our internal focus. The big cultural shift for us was to recognize that we are really here only to satisfy the customer."

Training for TQM

Pulling together for the "quality journey"

It began with a teller's wry remark at Texins Credit Union, Richardson, Texas. When the employee suggested staff hire the next teller, Branch Manager Anne Marcom laughed with the rest of them. Then she began to see possibilities in the suggestion that has since helped change the culture of the $605 million asset credit union.

Marcom, head of Texins' Campbell Road branch, gave her tellers the go-ahead. She sat in on interviews only to moderate and take notes.

The experiment that began as a wisecrack worked, and now the Campbell Road branch hires all tellers based on peer recommendations. Staff involved in employee interviews receive no special personnel management training. Rather, like all Texins Credit Union employees, they're steeped in the credit union's quality service emphasis. Their newfound empowerment has had a positive effect on member service as well as on the credit union's hiring and personnel policies.

Such are the characteristics of credit unions practicing total quality management (TQM). During the past decade, the philosophy of doing the right thing first and every time has taken the business world by storm. Credit unions, too, are embracing quality as a concept, a process, and a goal itself as defined by gurus like W. Edwards Deming, Philip Crosby, and Joseph Juran.

At the risk of shortchanging what's become a movement itself, TQM is an operational philosophy focusing on total customer satisfaction. "Customers" include not only credit union members, but employees, officers, and even vendors—anyone at the receiving end of a work process contributing to the continued operation and promotion of credit union service goals.

Recently, a growing number of institutions have adopted a quality approach to improve member service and keep a closer tab on the bottom line. Many already have found just how well it works.

"We began our move toward TQM about six years ago, with our strongest emphasis during the past 18 months," says Geri Dillingham, senior vice president of marketing for $568 million asset North Island Federal Credit Union, Chula Vista, Calif. "Now we invest more than $1 million annually in total quality instruction, including training, team incentives, recognition, and reward."

Staff and member surveys recently ranked North Island Federal high in terms of both employee and member satis-faction, two basic tenets of TQM. Dillingham says the quality movement has helped the credit union perform func-tions faster, more effectively, and with greater member ser-vice.

Central to TQM develop-ment, both at North Island Federal and other credit unions, has been the effective training of staff, executives, and board members in what could be the most profound personnel management revo-lution to affect the credit union movement.

"In training, total quality is at the forefront. It's vital to future credit union growth and development," says Harley Skjervem, vice presi-dent of CUNA's Human Re-source Development (HRD) Department.

Many credit unions agree, Skjervem says, and a growing number are taking a formal-ized approach to TQM. That means increased staff train-ing. And, like the teller hir-ing procedures at Texins Credit Union, that training sometimes takes unusual turns.

These days, more employ-ees at Texins are hired based on peer interview and recom-mendation, says George Pavelek, who, with true TQM egalitarianism, describes his position as "being involved with staff development and quality."

"It's a process that's mov-ing through our organization like flu through a kindergar-ten," Pavelek says. "Each new employee team comes up with a new twist. It all further re-fines the process."

The process of TQM has been active at Texins for about three years, but Pavelek will be the first to say it's not a control mechanism, mana-gerial function, or philosophy du jour.

We invest more than $1 million annually in total quality instruction, includ-ing training, team incen-tives, recognition, and re-ward."

—Geri Dillingham
North Island FCU

"We don't believe quality is controlled. You can control the work process, but quality is something that's deliv-ered," Pavelek says. "Quality means conforming to the cus-tomers' requirements. That's fundamental to its success."

If staff delivers service meeting or exceeding the de-sired requirement, paving the way for the next step, Pavelek describes it as "another step in the quality journey."

"There are as many ways to do total quality wrong as there are stars in the sky," Pavelek says. "It requires an enormous amount of educa-tion now and forever to sup-port this journey."

Texins' employee TQM training is a four-part cur-riculum that includes: 1) technical training about the credit union's various sys-tems; 2) skills training which focuses on the application of that technical knowledge; 3) basic staff development, in-cluding orientation and career management paths; and 4) quality education, intro-ducing employees to Texins' TQM philosophy and busi-ness style. Pavelek says such training is vital in helping the credit union pursue its goal: "When our organization can do what it does as well as or better than the world's best provider, then we've achieved world-class quality."

Part of the effort includes mixing employees from vari-ous departments and of dif-ferent levels into six strategic quality improvement teams (SQITs). The teams examine everything: staff develop-ment, recognition, measure-ment, innovation, teamwork, and benchmarking. Benchmarking is a TQM process of continually seeking and implementing the most effective methods.

In order to launch an effective quality journey, Pavelek says an employee needs to attend Texins' two two-day workshops devoted to quality education, QE 100 and QE 200. Established in the spring of 1992, the workshops provide basic TQM education and are required for all of Texins' 230 employees.

"There's an expectation and invitation for all staff to participate in these workshops," Pavelek says. "Every employee has to wrestle with whether we're creating a culture or if this is just another program that will run its course.

"But we have a credit union culture that's changing, and we need to bring these changes before our staff. We've created a culture in which all staff recognize not only the opportunity and need to be creative, but that there are systems in place to support that creativity."

That's the philosophy and focus of Texins' TQM development, Pavelek says. Increased and effective staff training is vital to support the function and evolve with the market it serves.

Downtrends in Training

Training is an integral part of TQM, but recent growth in credit union staff training has been flat at best. In some cases, expenditures actually have decreased, according to the findings of several *Credit Union Magazine* human resource surveys.

In 1990, credit unions of all asset sizes spent an average $13,319 on training, compared with $16,190 for the previous two years combined. By 1992, those numbers had flattened out in most categories, showing a significant drop among smaller credit unions.

The drop occurred in credit unions with less than $2 million in assets. Expenditures fell from $4,109 in 1990 to $1,068 in 1992. All other categories grew modestly, with the greatest growth coming in credit unions of $100 million or more in assets. In that open-ended category, training expenditures rose from $53,454 in 1990 to $76,561 in 1992.

In recent years, training budgets for all industries were cut an average 5%, according to the American Society for Training and Development (ASTD), with number of training hours declining 5% and the number of individu-

als trained 7%. In the financial services industry, 92% of all institutions suffered some level of cutbacks.

By comparison, credit unions' greatest training cuts were among smaller-asset institutions. All other expenditures have remained the same or risen slightly.

According to CUNA's Skjervem, a combination of a softening economy, the Persian Gulf war, and the presidential election affected credit unions' training expenditures.

"In training, total quality is at the forefront. It's vital to future credit union growth and development."

—Harley Skjervem, CUNA

"But we've noticed there may be more training dollars in the system this year because our first-quarter numbers are up," he says. "With the new administration and a better economy, we expect growth this year."

And TQM education will be a major focus for many credit unions, prompting CUNA's HRD Department to develop its first credit union TQM symposium. Scheduled for October in Memphis,

Tenn., the event will combine the views of quality experts with the experiences of credit unions currently building TQM programs. The symposium will culminate in an after-hours tour of Memphis-based Federal Express, a company known for service quality and the winner of the 1991 Malcolm Baldridge Award for quality.

Talking Quality

One executive with a good story to tell is Chris Lindelof, president/chief executive officer (CEO) of $63 million asset Cherry Point Federal Credit Union, Havelock, N.C.

The institution "began talking quality" in 1986, Lindelof says, and formalized its approach three years ago. In addition to investing $6,000 to $12,000 each year in quality training sessions, Cherry Point Federal strongly supports all types of training. The credit union leads North Carolina in Staff Training and Recognition (STAR) certification and is active in the Volunteer Achievement Program (VAP) and Certified Credit Union Executive (CCUE) program—programs CUNA and the leagues offer.

"I have an underlying value system that says the more training an employee gets, the more valuable the employee is," Lindelof says. "Theoretically, every training dollar goes to support quality service."

That makes training key to Cherry Point Federal's TQM effort, Lindelof says. Like Texins Credit Union, Cherry Point Federal focuses on improving service and achieving quality as defined by member satisfaction levels.

"We do not define quality; we cannot define quality. Only the member can define quality," Lindelof says. "You have to look at quality through members' eyes. That's where continuous process improvement comes into play."

Cherry Point Federal also appoints cross-vertical and cross-departmental employee teams to address issues and obstacles affecting service delivery. In the past few years, the credit union's seven teams have made 39 recommendations for process improvements. Management declined only three, due to cost or impracticality.

Diane Halverson, vice president of State Capitol Employees Credit Union, Madison, Wis., says her credit union's quality effort began five years ago with employee empowerment. However, it wasn't until last summer that management formally introduced the total quality concept to employees in eight half-day sessions. The $135 million asset credit union devoted $20,000 of its $50,000 training budget to TQM education and produces a quarterly quality newsletter.

"It's a slow process educating our staff of 80 while still conducting daily business," Halverson says. "We haven't changed a lot. We're still evolving."

On the other hand, $175 million asset Direct Federal Credit Union, Needham Heights, Mass., is deeply into its quality evolution. CEO David Breslin arrived from an executive post with meat packager Frank Perdue in 1985 to find a credit union struggling with a long list of problems. In 1986, Breslin began to follow the same quality route his former employer espoused.

"We were the first credit union in the nation and one of the first financial institutions to sign up with Philip Crosby & Associates," Breslin says. Breslin attended Crosby's Quality College in Winter Park, Fla., in 1986 and has since sent numerous management-level staff to follow the same path.

In addition, Direct Federal's entire staff go through a 40-hour quality training course evenly split between in-class and out-of-class exercises. The course is devoted to understanding Direct Federal's quality improvement process and applying it to service situations.

Breslin says the credit union spends up to $50,000 each year on quality training and development, "although the first few years ran closer to $100,000 each." The end result has been improved services and reduced expenses. That includes a reduction in staff from 88 employees in 1986 to 59 this year.

"Staff reduction isn't necessarily a goal of TQM, but I hope productivity is defined by the number of people required to do the same work or more over time," Breslin says.

Of the 59 staff members, 44 were recommended by their peers as qualifying for one of the three top quality performance awards the credit union offered in 1992. "We first started to see it all come together last year," Breslin says. "It's a long process, and credit unions and their boards need to realize that it may take four to five years to get everyone working in the same direction."

TQM truths

Lindelof agrees that TQM is not a quick fix. In fact, long-term commitment is one of the truths of TQM development. "Quality management is a long-range process and goal," he says. "It's an attitude, not a slogan. It's a way of life, not a program."

"There are as many ways to do total quality wrong as there are stars in the sky. It requires an enormous amount of education now and forever to support this journey."

—George Pavelek, Texins CU

Time is a component, no matter which TQM school of thought a credit union follows. So is personal commitment at all staff, management, and board levels. At Cherry Point Federal, Lindelof says three board members were involved with quality through their military base obligations, helping to spearhead the credit union's initial efforts. Since the program's establishment, several others have taken advantage of the credit union's quality training program.

"Our board went back and rewrote our credit union's mission statement to reflect our commitment to quality," Lindelof says.

Pavelek has a similar story at Texins Credit Union. Directors helped initiate and support TQM efforts, he says, but have taken a hands-off approach to implementation.

North Island Federal's board also is involved, but in a special way. President/CEO Mike Maslak sits on the board, and he's also one of 250 field examiners for the Malcolm Baldridge Award. Maslak's intimate knowledge of the quality process has helped the credit union achieve noteworthy results.

"TQM is the primary motivator in everything we do," says Chris Lamb, North Island Federal's senior vice president of planning and development. "We have a strong employee-focused service culture."

Part of that employee focus is the credit union's extensive training program, which includes specific quality service courses. Course content includes analyzing work processes; studying quality problem-solving tools, techniques, and actions; clarifying customer expectations and resolving complaints; and ensuring quality problem-solving process participation.

One of the biggest challenges, says Cathy Wallace, is providing quality training for all staff without impeding their ability to serve members. The vice president of training and development at North Island Federal notes that the credit union requires 30 hours of quality training for each staff member, including top executives, and 60 hours for middle management charged with facilitating the program.

"Every employee can earn a quality certificate for completing the program," says Lamb. "Since we started in November 1991, 80% of our 350 employees have been certified."

Like North Island Federal, most credit unions involved in TQM work hard at it. For others, however, it's just business as usual.

"Quality management is a long-range process and goal; it's not a quick fix. It's an attitude not a slogan. It's a way of life, not a program."

—Chris Lindelof
Cherry Point FCU

"TQM is pretty much a way of life for us, and it always has been," says Charlotte McNeal, CEO of Federal Express Credit Association Federal Credit Union, Memphis, Tenn. "It's a people world, and we're a service organization. That's [Federal Express CEO] Fred Smith's philosophy, period."

The credit union follows its corporate sponsor's lead, McNeal says, in its pursuit of quality training. Both entities have quality action teams that address various service and customer issues. Team leaders then meet with management to discuss results and recommend alternatives.

Like other credit unions, Federal Express Credit Association Federal surveys employees and members as a way to define direction and levels of service. Credit union employees even qualify for the corporate sponsor's Bravo Zulu awards for going above and beyond the call of duty in providing quality service.

"To me, quality is business as usual," explains McNeal. "I just took it for granted that everyone ought to be doing it."

From the direction many credit unions already have taken, that undoubtedly is the coming trend.

The Infrastructure for Total Quality Management

Joseph J. Haefner
Timothy J. Bartel

INTRODUCTION

"I think most of them are wasting their time. Not because they shouldn't emphasize quality, but because they don't know what they are doing." The well-known quality consultant Phil Crosby offered this observation when asked "do you think the industry (e.g. banking) is right to be placing all this emphasis on quality"[1] With Total Quality Management (TQM); even more-so. The result of "not knowing" what to do with TQM is examined in many recent articles about quality implementation failures. Studies by respected consulting firms indicate that less than one fourth of quality initiatives yield "tangible results."[2]

Given the difficulty in attaining "tangible results" from quality initiatives, a cadre of consultants are capitalizing on the confusion to market their own systems and methods. Some have taken up the banner against the much regarded TQM. Some are even touting "partial quality management" vs. total quality management; a contradiction in terms and a confounding of the progress made in recent years. This is unfortunate but predictable given the knowledge, long-term commitment, skill and experience domain necessary to successfully develop a TQM management system.

Implementing a TQM system is problematic not only because of the large knowledge-base, but also because it must address the fundamental difficulties of transforming an organization's philosophy, management structure, and technical expertise; "the infrastructure" as Secretary of Labor Robert Reich would say. Herein lies a major barrier confounding TQM. Lack of clear understanding of the infrastructure is why quality "tools" (statistics, SPC & etc.) and "methods" (Just in Time [JIT], Quality Function Deployment [QFD], and Problem Solving Models) are erroneously referred to as TQM. They are components of the infrastructure, not the infrastructure itself. Not knowing this difference is generating inability to sustain momentum in quality initiatives or TQM transition. Not knowing the components of the TQM system and how to integrate and deploy those components is causing some uninformed individuals to question whether TQM is a fad and whether TQM is dead. Those who refuse to unfurl their sails to the winds of change cater to this group.

Let us pose a simple comparison to demonstrate our conjecture. Imagine the difference between a computer program (the computer code) and a computer system. A computer program is similar to a quality tool or method. A computer system with its hardware equipment, databases, support staff, many software programs and procedures can be compared to the system of TQM. Now, imagine attempting to use a computer program without a computer system to support it. Herein lies the crux of the problem. In short, we have approached a sophisticated management system with a reductionist mentality. That is to say, we have tried to reduce a complex system into a few simple components. And, why not? It has been the essence of manufacturing, business and political thinking for decades. To be sure, reductionist thinking can appear to be somewhat successful in a noncompetitive, nondynamic environment. However, it cannot succeed in the current world environment. The obviousness of this lies in the previously referenced statistic: three out of four attempts at TQM do not yield any tangible results.

The purpose of this article, then, is to briefly examine the infrastructure of TQM. What does the system look like? What are the components of a TQM system? It is our desire to leave the reader, our customer, with an understanding of the infrastructure of TQM. We would also like to briefly comment on some fundamental steps necessary to begin understanding TQM.

TOTAL QUALITY MANAGEMENT

There are at least as many definitions of TQM as there are definitions of quality. However, TQM is simply involving all employees in an integrated, systems approach to fact-based decision-making and "breakthrough" improvement for the purpose of meeting or exceeding customer needs and expectations; hopefully delighting the customer. Breakthrough is defined as significant improvement, generally 50 percent or better improvements. Daily incremental improvements are also a component of TQM. As we shall see, TQM is designed to synthesize all aspects of organizational activity into purposeful strategies leading to dynamic organizational evolution to meet the needs of a changing market.

Before we look at the attributes of TQM we should first look at what a TQM system organizes and manages. There are at least five very fundamental domains from which strategic plans evolve.

They are profit, quality, delivery, cost, and human resources. The management of these domains define the success or failure of an organization. Let's consider these a moment. Without profit nothing can be pursued. Profit is what allows organizational survival. TQM espouses determining a way to profitably meet customers' needs. The catch is that customer needs drive the processes that produce the profits, not the other way around; hard-selling what can be profitable made.

There is also cost. As W. Edwards Deming says, there are knowable and unknowable costs. Knowable costs are those that can be put in an accounting ledger. Costs of this type also include the cost of trying to save money by purchasing cheap, low quality raw materials. Or, the cost of hiring cheap labor vs. investing in a current workforce. The adage "you get what you pay for" is not without meaning in this regard. Unknowable costs are those which cannot be put in accounting ledgers but which can determine the success or failure of a business. One cost may be loss of customers after years of providing shoddy products generated by cheap materials (or services). That practice can be successful when there is no competition.

However, when people have alternatives, they will naturally choose the best product or service for the best price. Another unknowable cost is the impact of a well-trained and motivated work force.

Delivery is efficiency of a product or service moving from a raw material stage to delivery to the customer. This concern appears as "cycle time reduction" in process improvement strategies. It includes all activities from suppliers, through processes, up to and including the consumption of a product or service (particularly in the service sector). This is the domain of Just in Time (JIT). In manufacturing it would tend to focus on removing "dead space" between production activities. In service, removing "dead space" is also desired. Cycle time reduction could include reduction of waiting time in the health care industry or reducing the time to process applications.[3]

Quality is defined as the "goodness of results as perceived by the customer."[4] In the past, quality and cost have been interpreted as mutually exclusive. That is to say that providing quality products or service always costs more. Hence, quality was considered contrary to quick, inexpensive, production. However,

this is not the case. It does not cost more to provide quality in a product or service. It has been documented many times that quality improvement creates efficient systems; and usually with substantial cost savings.

Human resources would be the management of all aspects of developing and maintaining the human element. That would include safety, training, career development, health and morale. Thus Deming's concept of profound knowledge must be understood, particularly, the theories of knowledge and psychology. These define the need for human self-actualization as described in current books about learning organizations.[5]

These five domains significantly interact and influence one another. The power of TQM is how it integrates and aligns their management. It stands to reason that TQM is measured by the efficacy of their integration in strategic goals; excellence of daily management; and cross-functionality. We can also infer from Deming's teachings that not only must these domains be managed well independently, they must also be in sync operationally *and philosophically.*

TQM INFRASTRUCTURE

We have just alluded to the principle infrastructure of TQM: strategic planning, daily management, and cross-functional management. Following is a tree diagram showing the TQM domains and some of the technical attributes. We will proceed to examine those.

Strategic Planning[6] is also called *Hoshin Kanri* by the Japanese and "integrated planning" in the U.S. It consists of four well-defined procedures which encompass the Plan-Do-Check-Act (PDCA) model. They are:

I. Strategy Formulation

1. Review previous year's result

2. Analyze internal and external business environment

   a. Internal:

      Malcolm-Baldrige assessment or ISO 9000 audit

   b. External:

      environmental scans, market research, etc.

```
                              ┌─────────────────────┐
                              │ Annual              │
                              │ Strategic Goals     │
                              ├─────────────────────┤
              ┌────────────┐  │ Vertical            │
              │ Stategic   │  │ Business Plan       │
              │ Business   │──│ Integration         │
              │ Planning   │  ├─────────────────────┤
              └────────────┘  │ Fact Based Tools    │
                              │ & Review System     │
                              ├─────────────────────┤
                              │ 3-5 Year Vision     │
                              └─────────────────────┘
                              ┌─────────────────────┐
                              │ Customer            │
                              │ Information         │
                              │ QFD, Surveys, Etc.  │
┌──────────────┐             ├─────────────────────┤
│ Vision,      │ ┌─────────┐ │ Horizontal          │
│ Mission      │ │ Cross   │ │ Planning &          │
│ &            │─│Functional│─│ Systems Control     │
│ Customer     │ │Management│ ├─────────────────────┤
└──────────────┘ └─────────┘ │ Information         │
                              │ Systems             │
                              ├─────────────────────┤
                              │ Audit               │
                              └─────────────────────┘
                              ┌─────────────────────┐
                              │ Employee            │
                              │ Involvement         │
                              ├─────────────────────┤
                              │ 7 Quality Tools     │
              ┌────────────┐  ├─────────────────────┤
              │ Daily Process│ │ 7 Step             │
              │ Management  │─│ Improvement         │
              └────────────┘  │ Process (Root       │
                              │ Cause Analysis)     │
                              ├─────────────────────┤
                              │ Standardization     │
                              │ & Continuous        │
                              │ Improvement         │
                              └─────────────────────┘
```

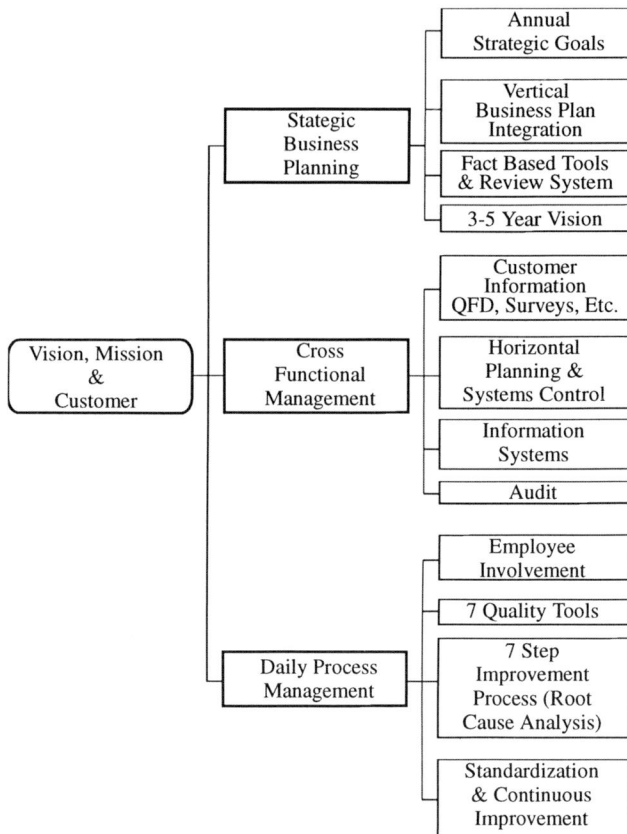

Figure 1. **TQM Components Tree Diagram**

3. Customer analysis

   a. Quality function deployment

   b. Surveys, focus groups, complaints

4. Competitive information

5. Strategy formulation

Formulating Annual Plans reviews the previous year's annual plan results, examines internal and external environments, analyzes customer needs, analyzes competitive information, and determines a strategy for the next Annual Business Plan. The result of this step is to identify Key Strategic Objectives (KSOs)[7] for the year[8] which support the long term direction of the organization.

II. Drafting of an Annual Business Plan

   1. Identify areas vital to the achievement of KSOs:

      Determine key result areas, KRAs

   2. Determine measures for the KRAs:

      Define key result measures, KRMs

   3. Identify major improvement opportunities, MIOs:

      Assign target values for MIOs

Drafting the Annual Plan involves identifying Key Strategic Areas (KSAs), determining Key Result Measures (KRMs), and identifying Major Improvement Opportunities (MIOs). Targets for improvement are then assigned. This component of business planning is important because it identifies where improvements can be made; and how to measure the progress toward those improvements.

III. Developing the Plan

   1. Develop means (action plans) for each MIO:

      Determine how the targets will be accomplished

   2. "Cascade" the target and means down through the organization

a. Develop
   functional action
   plans

b. Identify areas
   targeted for "root
   cause analysis"

3. Finalize action plans

a. Assess internal
   resources

b. Assess financial
   impact for human
   resource
   development:

      determine
      training costs

4. Evaluate technology
   capabilities

5. Final approval

Developing the Annual Plan is where the Plan is delivered down through the organization to functional areas so they can determine how to accomplish the MIOs. This is a critical step of the *Hoshin Kanri* or policy deployment models from Japan as this guarantees the linkage between strategic plans and functional goals. This step involves much communication and fine-tuning of the Annual Plan. Budgetary considerations are paramount. Any quality or technical training would be determined in this step. This is appropriately where quality skill training needs are determined.

IV. Implementing and Checking the Progress of the Annual Business Plan

1. Execute the plan

2. Evaluate plan results
   a. Periodic reviews
   b. Corrective actions
   c. Annual
      evaluation

Finally, the Plan is implemented and checks of progress occur periodically to verify how well the plan is going. If some areas are not meeting the targets of their action plan an evaluation is conducted. Shortcomings in achieving goals are always input for the next year's annual plan.

The strategic element of TQM is what gives TQM the "Total." Without strategic planning there is no TQM. However, that does not imply that quality activities are not important or successful. It must be weighed carefully whether to pursue TQM or simply Quality Improvement (QI). If TQM is pursued, the first strategic planning cycles usually take from 18 to 24 months. After that, the planning cycle becomes annual. Development of a rudimentary TQM system is said to take three to five years.

Daily Management is the creation and maintenance of stable, predictable, efficient operations. In this part of the TQM infrastructure, employees and managers determine critical processes and concentrate on standardizing, controlling and improving those processes. It is often said that daily management must be established before the other components of TQM can be fully functional. For example, creating a Just-In-Time system (JIT is a crossfunctional component) is very difficult if operations are not predictable and dependable.

Critical processes are important tasks or procedures which determine the success of an organization. They directly affect the customer. The attributes of critical processes[9] are:

1. They are few, usually 5–10.

2. They are vertically and horizontally linked.

3. They can be flow-charted or mapped.

4. They are measurable.

5. Critical processes can be improved.

Stability and predictability of critical processes are essential.

The sequence of activities for determining critical processes is as follows:

1. Identify your major customers:

    Internal and external

2. Identify your customers' needs:

    Work from the customers' point of view

3. Define the products (process outputs) provided to meet customer needs.

4. Determine which processes are key to provide customer needs.

When critical processes are determined, standardization and control may be pursued. The evolution of establishing process stability and predictability is shown using what Dr. Joseph M. Juran calls the Juran Trilogy. It shows the phases of establishing process stability and predictability.

Moving through the Juran Trilogy scenario using process engineering or root cause analysis results in process stabilization, standardization and quality control to "hold the gains." When this has occurred, employees have a predictable process and can begin Standardize-Do-Check-Act (SDCA). This would be what Deming would refer to as "continuous improvement." We believe that this is where quality circles and self-directed work teams begin.

Tools and methods for accomplishing process predictability would be statistical process control (SPC), the 7

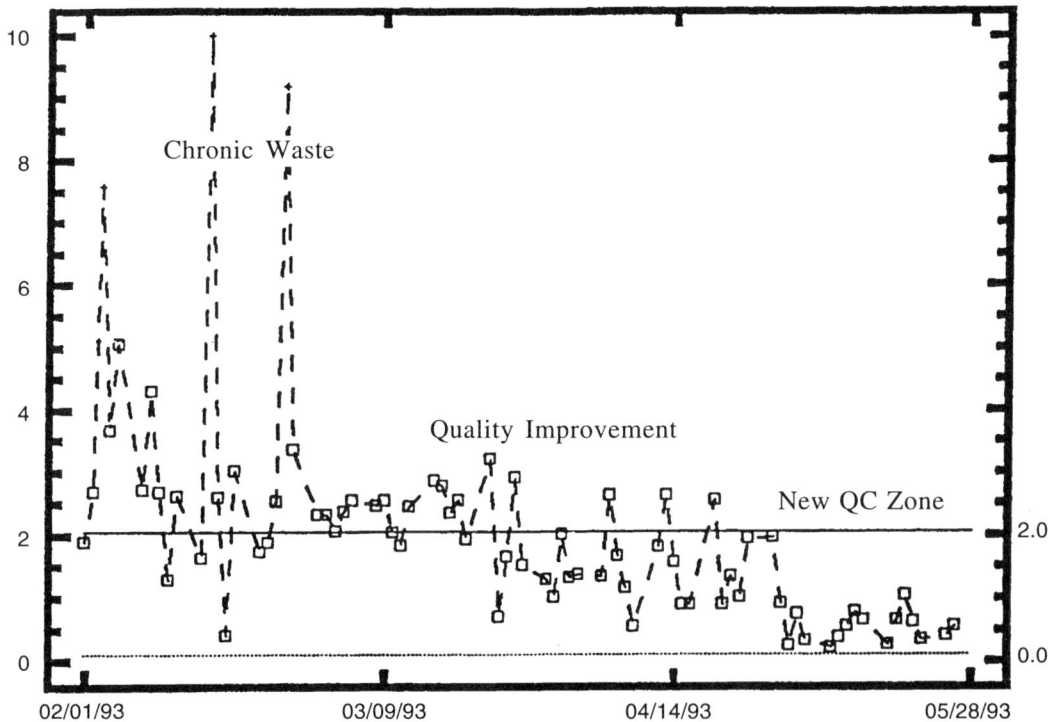

Figure 2. **The Juran Trilogy**

Step Improvement Process, worker improvement teams and quality control systems. You may recall that in the early 1980s these were the focus of the quality improvement in U.S. industry. Many of those initiatives failed. They failed because the infrastructure to support, integrate and sustain those activities was not understood and not in place.

Cross-Functional Management (CFM) focuses on activities which cross departmental and functional boundaries. It includes quality, profit, cost, delivery, and human resources. Supporting functions include supplier relations, internal audit, information systems, Just in Time and support activities involved in acquiring consumer/customer information.

Deming shows the following cross-functional view (figure 3) of an organization (or system, as he calls it).[10]

The objective of CFM is to coordinate the activities of all the functional units of an entire system. One goal of CFM is to remove anything, product or service, which would create problems for internal or external customers of that system. The most obvious concern would be anything which is not consistent with customer needs. Naturally, suppliers are an integral part of this TQM domain. If they provide poor product or service, problems may result in every functional unit of the system, including with the customer.

Another goal is to fully understand how every critical

process of an operation relates to every other process. For this, new emerging techniques are evolving. The most comprehensive is called Quality Function Deployment (QFD). It, combined with sophisticated surveying and consumer analysis, helps organizations to learn what customers' needs are, how to provide those needs, how all internal functions relate to provide customer needs and how the competition is doing. This is exhibited in an A-1 Matrix.

The A-1 Matrix is often referred to as the "House of Quality." As you can see from the figure on the next page,[11] it contains customer requirements and importance rating (customer needs), quality characteristics (how the needs may be addressed), a

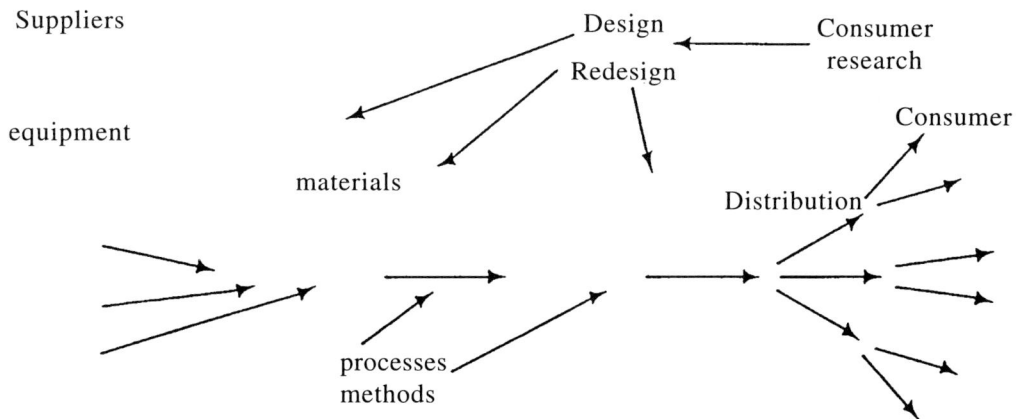

Figure 3. **Adapted from W.E. Deming's Concept of a System**

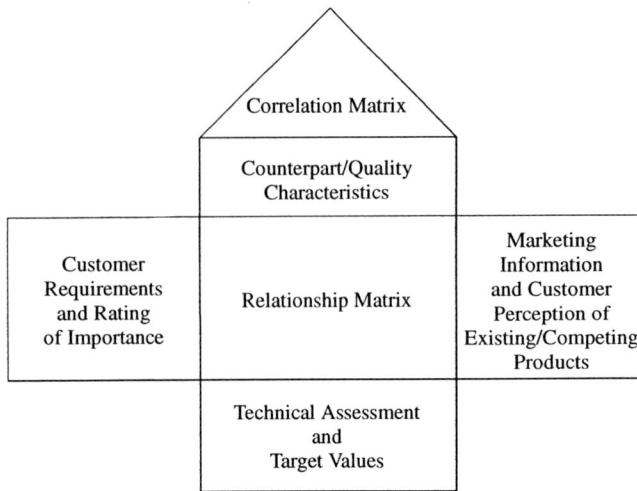

Figure 4. **A-1 Matrix** *

correlation matrix of potential positive or negative interaction of quality characteristic, marketing information, technical comparisons and how all of those elements are related.

The A-1 Matrix, however, is merely the base matrix. Associated with the A-1 Matrix is the "Matrix of Matrices." The Matrix of Matrices shows the real cross-functional power of QFD. Virtually every functional activity of an organization can be related to the A-1 Matrix through the Matrix of Matrices. For example, Matrix B-2 is the cost deployment main chart. It compares an organization to competitors on such

items as selling price, manufacturing costs and market share. The vertical column would contain these items. The horizontal row would contain the company and competitors.

A particularly important matrix is the G-6 Matrix. It is a list of parts (or components) of service and how they relate to control methods, instruction, procedures, etc. The G-6 Matrix shows the potential of QFD. QFD starts with customer needs and ends up with standardized procedures for controlling those processes which directly contribute to the "quality" desired by the customer. Every functional system between the A-1 and

G-6 matrix can be related. That is what is meant by cross-functional.

To create a cross-functional management system some organizations establish committees or appoint vice-presidents responsible for human resources, quality, delivery, and profit/cost. It would be their task to work with one another, crossfunctionally, to increase system effectiveness by coordinating the interface of the individual areas. So, for example, human resources would have the goal of maintaining a low turnover rate among employees. This would support both the delivery and profit/cost function by reducing the amount of on-the-job training. It would also help maintain a greater employee expertise level for the organization. Cost would be affected. Low turnover would result in less cost for training and less cost due to inexperience.

STARTING THE TRANSFORMATION

Given this picture of TQM, it is not surprising that many companies have had problems showing tangible results for quality efforts. The TQM knowledge base, methods, tools, business planning, cus-

---

* Used with permission from *Quality Function Deployment,* GOAL/QPC's Research Report, Copyright ©
1989 GOAL/QPC, 13 Branch Street, Methuen MA 01844–1953.

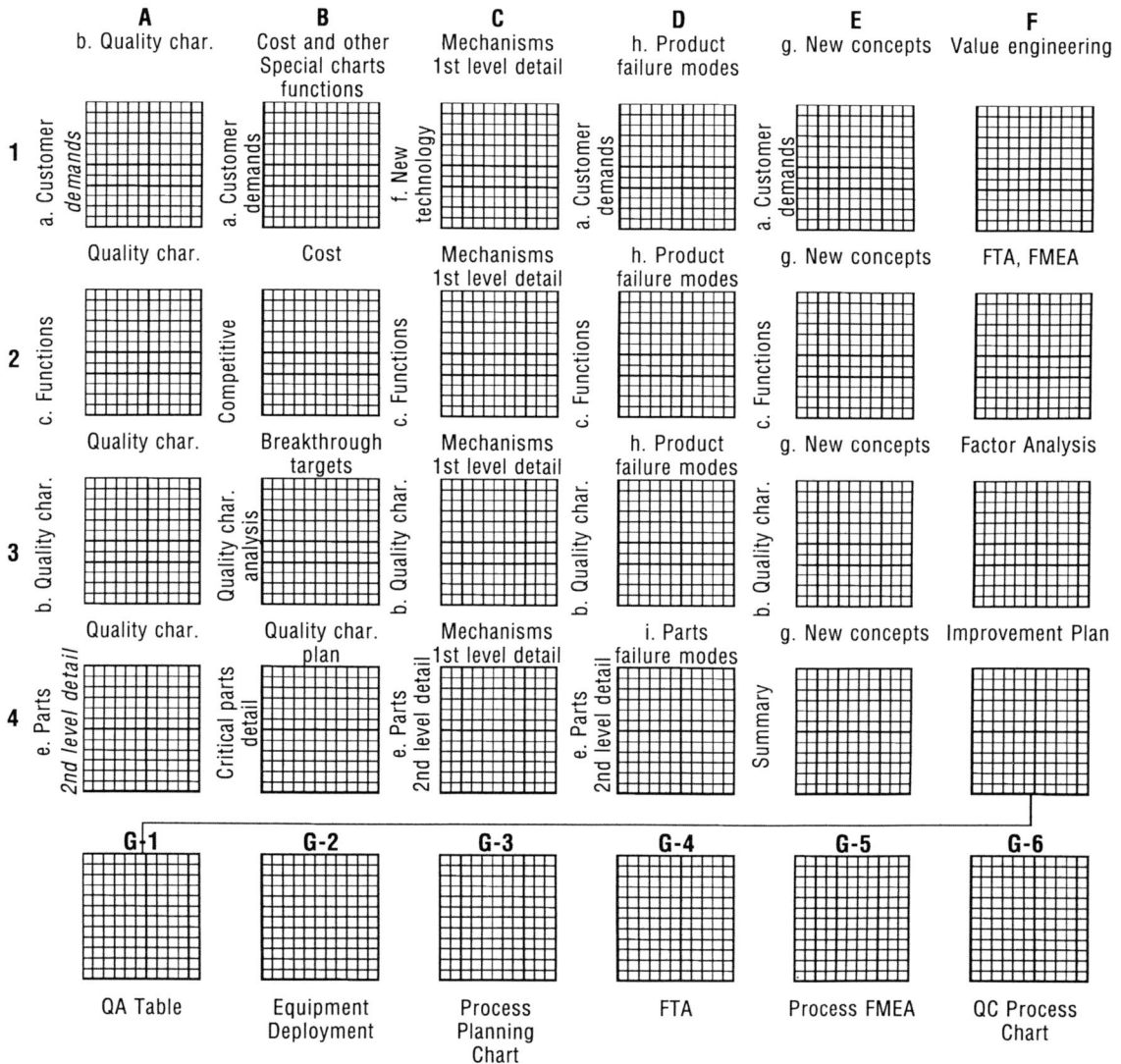

Figure 5. **Matrix of Matrices***

tomer orientation and employee support mechanisms are very large. What are executives left with in the face of this system of TQM? One can envision the potential confusion. What consultant does one chose? How should training be conducted? Who should be in training? To which quality guru should we pay homage? How much planning is needed before real quality improvement projects are begun? What is our innate insecurity and how does it limit our acceptance of TQM? These are all issues

---

* Reprinted with permission from *Better Designs in Half the Time,* Copyright © 1989 Bob King, GOAL/QPC, 13 Branch Street, .Methuen MA 01844–1953.

which have significant ramifications on the degree of success of a quality initiative.

Where, then, does one start when beginning a quality transformation? We would like to recommend the following steps:

1. When Dr. Deming began instructing the Japanese in the early 1950s, he introduced the Shewhart Cycle, more commonly known as PDCA. The cycle in simplified terms entails Planning the activity, Doing it, formally Checking (Studying the results of the activity), and Acting on the findings. The first essential task is to adopt a Plan-Do-Check-Act attitude and modus operandi. It is, after all, the first fundamental transformation model. The alternative is to end up in the Do-Act mode or the Plan-Do mode. Neither provides sufficient data-based feedback from which to determine the effectiveness of the Plan or Do phases. In a crisis this can evolve into Do-Do management.

2. The next task is to acquire adequate knowledge. This must include: what is TQM; what are the domains of TQM; what are the tools and methods of TQM; and what tools, techniques, and methods are essential to begin? Most important is to acquire enough knowledge to pick a good transformational model. Picking the wrong model, one not founded in an understanding of the components of TQM, can cause an organization to waste years trying to adopt a TQM system of management. The American Society for Quality Control and GOAL/QPC offer several books on transformational models.

3. Be prepared to continue learning. Reference the fact that some world- class companies (and Malcolm-Baldrige winning companies) require training of every employee every year. You can see by all we have discussed that there is a very large learning curve.

4. Carefully, choose how much quality improvement. Know that understanding the 7 Quality Tools and the 7 Step Improvement Process is mandatory. If the choice is to be ambitious and attempt TQM strategic planning, a good transformation model (again) is crucial. We recommend Goal/QPC's "Total Quality Master Plan" and the "Integrated Planning Model" as must reading. It should be noted that with a good transformation model, many many pitfalls can be avoided.

5. Learn Dr. Deming's concepts and philosophies. In particular are his teachings about "systems" and "variation." In general his philosophies get at the essence of human motivation, social dynamics, and psychology. Aside from Deming, it is also becoming evident that some knowledge of the socio-technical impacts of transformation should be understood.[12] Moving from our current management system to a TQM management system is not merely a linear change of infrastructure. It is also a social system change. Social system changes always involve contradictions in expected behavior and habits. These contradictions create stress, tension and conflict. One recent Deming Award-winning company lost many good employees due to this.

CONCLUSION

It has been argued that TQM is a fad whose days are done. This, we believe, is definitely not the case. There are nevertheless logistical concerns which must be addressed before successful TQM can evolve. First, there is a lack of experience in root cause analysis and process engineering. This would include knowledge and experience in problem solving and the application of basic statistical methodologies. The reason tangible results are not forthcoming in quality initiatives, our experience has shown, is due to this. Good training combined with experience will help to overcome this. As the quality expert Kaoru Ishikawa has stated "quality begins and ends with training."

Second, there is a significant lack of knowledge about the TQM infrastructure. Many, many organizations are claiming to be doing TQM. Many organizations have claimed to have "tried" TQM and it doesn't work. In most cases, the claim of "doing TQM" or having "tried TQM" cannot be true. These claims are based on using methods and tools which are components of the TQM system: reductionist thinking. As we indicated earlier, components of TQM are not TQM. Therefore, SPC is not TQM, employee involvement is not TQM, problem solving is not TQM, and continuous improvement is not TQM.

Third, without the strategic business planning process linked to the other components, the T in TQM is missing. This deficiency must be overcome.

We have just completed examining the infrastructure of TQM. It is very comprehensive. The large learning curve can be restrictive and time consuming. Nevertheless, this cannot be construed as the end of TQM. Rather, our current situation must be perceived for what it is: the expanding of our knowledge and awareness, and the growth of our experience and ability. We are, in reality, at the moment when our second wind kicks in.

---

1. Phil Crosby, "A Conversation with Philip Crosby," *Bank Marketing,* April 1991, p. 22.
2. Oren Harari, "Ten Reasons Why TQM Doesn't Work," *Management Review,* January 1993. pps. 33–38.
3. Two Rochester Institute of Technology and *USA Today* 1993 Quality Crystal team recipients earned recognition by reducing application cycle time; A University of Wisconsin project reduced graduate school admissions cycle time; CUNA Service Group reduced credit card application cycle time and, as a result, earned for their customer credit union.
4. From lecture notes of Professor Mark Finster, University of Wisconsin Graduate School of Business. Professor Finster has been instrumental in clarifying the philosophy, methods, tools and applications which are components of a TQM system.
5. For more information on Deming's concepts of Profound Knowledge see chapter four of his most recent book *The New Economics.* Also, see Peter Senge's *The Fifth Discipline.*
6. GOAL/QPC, "Integrated Planning Model," 13 Branch Street, Methuen, MA. 1992.
7. KSO = objectives critical to the success of the strategic plan
   KRA = key areas important to the strategic plan; e.g. functional areas, quality, cost, customer service, delivery, and productivity
   KRM = what each MIO is measured against
   MIO = specific processes, projects or business actions most important to the success of the KSO or KRA

8. Please note that the Malcolm-Baldrige National Quality Award focuses on the internal features of an organization. The reason some of these award recipients have done poorly in business is because this award does not focus on competitive issues, external business/economic issues, or other non-internal organizational factors. It is, therefore, a poor predictor of business success. However, focus on those internal organizational activities and systems which *contribute* to quality and customer satisfaction.

9. Collett, Demott & Moran, "Introduction to Critical Processes," GOAL/QPC, 1992.

10. W. Edwards Deming, *The New Economics for Industry, Government, Education,* Massachusetts Institute of Technology Center for Advanced Engineering Study, Cambridge, MA, 1993.

11. Bob King, *Better Designs in Half the Time,* GOAL/QPC, 1989.

12. For additional information see Lawrence M. Miller's *Design for Total Quality.*

TQM ASSOCIATIONS
AND AWARDS

Since the advent of TQM, consulting groups have mobilized to offer training seminars and packages. Nearly every major city in the country has served as host to a TQM seminar. In the last decade, numerous local quality associations have emerged, and older established quality organizations became more active. Notable national organizations include:

- ASQC (American Society for Quality Control)
  Publishes TQM-related books, audio, and videotapes.
  611 East Wisconsin Ave., P.O. Box 3005, Milwaukee, WI, 53201
  (414) 272-8575

- GOAL\QPC
  Engages in research, publishing, and education via seminars.
  13 Branch Street, Methuen, MA 01844
  (508) 685-3900

Both organizations serve as excellent resources.

The coveted Malcolm Baldrige National Quality Award was established in 1987 by the U.S. government. This is the most prestigious business award in the country. Candidates for the award are judged in seven categories, in the following order: customer satisfaction, quality results, human resource utilization, quality assurance of products and services, leadership, planning for quality, information, and analysis. This quality award cannot be won by a non-profit organization, like a credit union, but it has been won by credit union-sponsoring organizations, including AT&T and Federal Express.

The Rochester Institute of Technology and *USA Today* Quality Cup Competition for Employees Improvement Teams was established to demonstrate the importance of employees in the quality movement.

SUMMARY OF TERMS

As you venture into the exciting and vast world of quality, you'll run into a variety of terms and concepts with which you may or may not be familiar. Because many of these terms have different interpretations, quality consultants suggest that each organization devise its own glossary of terms so that the intended definition is understood by all.

This is not that type of glossary. This is simply a listing of some common terms and concepts to guide you in your discovery of quality.

ASQC
American Society for Quality Control, headquartered in Milwaukee, Wisconsin, was established in 1946 to improve and maintain the quality of World War II defense materials. ASQC today is involved in a variety of professional, educational, and informational programs that reflect the changing demands of American business and industry.

Baldrige Award
The Malcolm Baldrige National Quality Award was established by the U.S. Congress in 1987, in honor of the secretary of commerce under President Reagan, who sought to encourage competitiveness of American companies. It is a prestigious honor awarded to those who demonstrate exemplary performance in Total Quality Management.

Bell curve
Normal distribution of data in which data points gravitate toward a mean or average and taper symmetrically on both sides.

Benchmarking
According to H. James Harrington, author of *Business Process Improvement*, benchmarking is "the act of systematically defining the best systems, processes, procedures, and practices." One organization, to improve its processes, may use benchmarking to compare its performance to that of an exemplary organization.

Breakthrough   Improvement of performance to an unprecedented level of quality.

Cause-and-Effect Diagram   Also known as the "fishbone" diagram. Developed by Dr. K. Ishikawa, it's a quality tool used to identify all possible causes and effects of a given problem.

Checksheet   An easy-to-use form for collecting and recording occurrences or locations of some phenomenon or activity. It is a way to display data to reveal underlying patterns.

Common Causes   Causes that are normally part of the process all the time and affect all outcomes of the process.

Control Chart   A run chart with upper and lower control limits. This helps to determine the process' stability and to identify special causes of variation in the process.

Critical Work Processes   The most important processes an organization needs to do to manage its business. Types of processes include serving both internal and external customers and the specific products or services that are offered.

Customer   A customer is anyone who is affected by a process or the results of a process (product or service).

Customer Satisfaction   Usually customer/member satisfaction is defined by meeting or exceeding a customer's expectations. Juran, in his book, *Juran on Leadership for Quality,* defines product and customer satisfaction as "a result achieved when product features respond to customer needs."

Deming Prize   Japanese award named after Dr. W. Edwards Deming in 1950. It is bestowed annually upon individuals and teams.

Empowerment	Giving people power and responsibility over their jobs. William C. Byham, in his book *Zapp! The Lightning of Empowerment*, illustrates, through a contemporary fable, how managers can effectively empower people and get results.
External Customer	An external customer is anyone who is affected by a given process, product, or service, and who is not part of the company that produces it. External customers in a credit union include: members and potential members, credit union leagues, the government, the financial industry as a whole, and the community. Some credit unions refer to external customers as business partners.
Flowchart	One of the many quality tools used to study, standardize, and improve processes. It offers a visual representation of the inputs, steps, and results of a given process.
GOAL/QPC	GOAL/QPC was founded in 1978 in Massachusetts as a regional effort to expand jobs in the area. GOAL/QPC shares its knowledge of cutting-edge research through its courses, publications, and training materials, and tailors its research knowledge to help other organizations adapt TQM methods to fit their own needs.
Histogram	A bar graph used to illustrate the distribution of data.
Hoshin Kanri	The Japanese term for strategic business planning. It involves designing and deploying annual organizational breakthrough plans involving all employees. The plans are developed through a communication method called "catchball" which occurs between all levels of the organization.
Input-Process-Output	The three phases of a system, also known as IPO. All phases need to be understood to have a high-quality predictable outcome.

Internal Customer   One who is affected by a process/product and is a part of the company that produces it. A credit union's internal customers, also called business partners, include the board of directors and staff who work together to reach the credit union's mission and vision. A payroll department's internal customers include each staff member who receives a paycheck. A new member service representative might serve a loan officer when he or she sends the new member to the loan department to refinance a home.

ISO   International Standards Organization is a specialized international agency comprised of 91 countries. It was set up with the purpose of developing worldwide standards to facilitate the international exchange of quality goods and services.

ISO 9000   ASQC explains the ISO 9000 Series Standards as, "international standards on quality management and quality assurance...They can be used by manufacturing and service industries alike. These standards were developed to effectively document the quality system elements to be implemented in order to maintain an efficient quality system in your company."

JIS   Japanese Industrial Standards. The JIS marking system has a standard for statistical quality control and quality assurance. If merchandise bears the JIS mark, it means that the merchandise has obtained this high standard. To qualify, a JIS standard factory needs to have made the merchandise.

JUSE   Union of Japanese Scientists and Engineers. A private organization formed by engineers and scholars in 1946 to improve the quality of Japanese exports. They did this by researching and implementing quality control methods.

Kaizen	Japanese management concept meaning "continuous, never-ending improvement" involving everyone in the workplace. It is an important element in understanding the difference between the Japanese process-oriented approach and the innovation and results-oriented thinking in the West.
Leadership	All of the quality thinkers place a great emphasis on the significance of leadership and management in any quality effort. Peter Senge, author of *The Fifth Discipline: The Art & Practice of the Learning Organization,* redefines the leader's role as designer, steward, and teacher. He claims leaders are "responsible for building organizations where people continually expand their capabilities to understand complexity, clarify vision, and improve shared mental models–that is, they are responsible for learning." (p. 340)
Mission Statement	Each quality team needs to write a project mission statement for every project. A good guide is to answer the question, "Why are we working on this project?"
Multi-voting	A method of voting to determine the item(s) of the highest priority for the group.
Nominal Group Process (NGP)	A way to generate and prioritize ideas from a group. Each team member is asked for ideas on solving a problem or issue. The ideas are recorded on a flip chart. The team leader should continue to ask each team member until all of the ideas are exhausted. Then all members are asked to vote on their favorite 5–9 ideas on a piece of paper. Based on the votes, the number one idea is chosen.
Operational Definitions	Defining what a term is and how you are going to measure that term.

Paradigm

A pattern or example. Paradigms have been called "rules and regulations," or the ways in which we see the world. A paradigm can have the effect of binding us to old patterns of behavior. Or, if we recognize our present paradigms, we can look beyond them and begin to envision the future.

Pareto Diagram

Bar graph used to illustrate data classifications arranged in descending order from left to right. This chart points out the biggest problems so the organization can concentrate on those first. Developed by Dr. J. Juran to illustrate the vital few and trivial many (commonly known as the 80/20 rule).

PDCA (PDSA)

Plan–Do–Check–Act Cycle (or, Plan–Do–Study–Act Cycle) is also known as the Deming Cycle or the Shewhart Cycle. Deming uses it to illustrate the essential concept of continuous improvement. According to Deming, an organization must constantly and forever improve its system of production and service.

Principles

Steven Covey, in his book, *The Seven Habits of Highly Effective People,* calls principles "guidelines for human conduct that are proven to have enduring, permanent value." Most TQM theorists place principles at the foundation of a quality transformation. Many claim that the principles of an organization must be written down as a blueprint to encourage empowered decision-making and progress toward quality.

Process

A set of operational systems and subsystems that transform and add value to inputs.

Process Improvement

The continuous endeavor to learn about the cause system of problems in a process and to use this knowledge to change the process in order to reduce variation and complexity and to improve customer satisfaction.

Project Team

A group of people who study the work processes needing improvement and work together to find permanent solutions to those problems.

QC Circles

QC Circles were formalized in Japan by Kaoru Ishikawa. They were designed as self-directed groups of workers who voluntarily came together to improve processes. These groups' goals were to contribute to an organization's overall total quality effort. QC Circles, due to their effectiveness, became very prevalent in Japan. Western businesses have adapted Ishikawa's QC Circle methodology into quality circles and quality control circles.

Quality Control

Kaoru Ishikawa, in his book *What Is Quality Control?*, defines this concept as follows: "To practice quality control is to develop, design, produce, and service a quality product which is most economical, most useful, and always satisfactory to the customer." In this book, Ishikawa sites the Japanese Industrial Standards (JIS) definition as, "a system of production methods which economically produces quality goods or services meeting the requirements of consumers. Modern quality control utilizes statistical methods and is often called statistical quality control." (p. 44)

Quality Improvement

According to Juran, quality improvement is the organized creation of beneficial change.

Quality

Many thinkers in the quality movement hesitate to give a definitive definition of this word. Niki Nicastro McCuistion, co-author of *The Quality Sales Leadership System for Today's Financial Executive,* offers this suggestion: "Quality is a long-term commitment to continuous improvement; it is recognizing that to do more than just survive in today's competitive marketplace, we must not only meet but also exceed our customers' and members' expectations."

Rework

The extra work involved with having to redo a project or step of a process because the objective was not clearly defined, a defect was found in the final product, or because the customer was not satisfied.

Special Causes

Causes that are not present in the process all the time but arise because of unusual circumstances.

Stable Process

A process which contains no special causes of variation. Only stable processes can be intentionally improved.

Standardization

Striving to do the same things, the same way, all the time, so the customer will always receive a product that is statistically the same.

Strategic Plan

A strategic plan is a blueprint that an organization designs to guide it toward its long-term goals and objectives.

Teams

One quality goal is to have all employees work together as if they were one big team. Therefore, by using smaller teams to instigate quality, you are following a quality principle, as well as drawing on the resources of many people rather than on one single person.

Vision

Credit unions need to have a long-term goal to strive for. One way of writing a vision statement is to answer the question "Where do we want to be in the future?"

RECOMMENDED STUDY

On Quality

Baldrige Award Winning Quality: How to Interpret the Malcolm Baldrige Award Criteria, by Mark Graham Brown

"The Infrastructure For Total Quality Management," by Haefner and Bartel

Total Quality, by Dan Ciampa

Deming

The New Economics, by W. Edwards Deming

Out of the Crisis, by W. Edwards Deming

The Deming Management Method, by Mary Walton

The Man Who Discovered Quality, by Andrea Gabor

Dr. Deming: The American Who Taught the Japanese About Quality, by Rafael Aguayo

The Deming of America: The Overview of Deming's Theory of Management (videotape), by Petty Consulting Productions

Crosby

Quality Is Free: The Art of Making Quality Certain, by Philip B. Crosby

Running Things: The Art of Making Things Happen, by Philip B. Crosby

Juran

Juran on Leadership for Quality: An Executive Handbook, by J.M. Juran

Juran on Planning for Quality, by J.M. Juran

Juran on Quality by Design: The New Steps for Planning Quality into Goods and Services, by J.M. Juran

Quality Control Handbook, by J.M. Juran, Frank M. Gryna, Jr., and R.S. Bingham, Jr.

On Continuous Improvement

KAIZEN: The Key to Japan's Competitive Success, by Masaaki Imai

Business Process Improvement: The Breakthrough Strategy for Total Quality, Productivity, and Competitiveness, by James H. Harrington

On Strategic Planning

Hoshin Kanri: Policy Deployment for Successful TQM, by Yoji Akao

"Integrated Planning Model," by GOAL/QPC Research Committee

On Quality Control

What Is Total Quality Control? The Japanese Way, by Kaoru Ishikawa

On Leadership

Principle-Centered Leadership, by Stephen R. Covey

The 7 Habits of Highly Effective People: Powerful Lessons in Personal Change, by Stephen R. Covey

Total Quality, by Ernest C. Huge

Managing Quality: The Strategic and Competitive Edge, by David A. Garvin

"Executive Leadership: Instituting a Quality Evolution," by Joseph J. Haefner

Leadership Is an Art, by Max De Pree

Driving Fear out of the Workplace, by Kathleen D. Ryan and Daniel Oestreich

Zapp! The Lightning of Empowerment: How to Improve Productivity, Quality and Employee Satisfaction, by William C. Byham and Jeff Cox

The Fifth Discipline: The Art and Practice of the Learning Organization, by Peter M. Senge

Oh! The Places You'll Go! by Dr. Seuss

On Tools and Methods

The Team Handbook, by Peter R. Scholtes

The Memory Jogger, by Michael Brassard, GOAL/QPC

The Memory Jogger Plus+ – Featuring the Seven Management and Planning Tools, by Michael Brassard, GOAL/QPC

Hoshin Planning: The Developmental Approach, by Bob King

Introduction to Critical Processes, by Casey Collett, Joann DeMott and John Moran

Understanding Statistical Process Control, by Donald Wheeler and David Chambers

"7 Step Improvement Process: Overview Document," by Joe Haefner, Shelly Hornback, Thea Hefty and Andrea Hughes; CUNA Service Group, 5710 Mineral Point Road, Madison, WI 53705

The Human Side of Quality

Incredibly American: Releasing the Heart of Quality, by Marilyn Zuckerman and Lewis J. Hatala

Incredibly American: Releasing the Heart of Quality (audiotape), by Marilyn Zuckerman and Lewis J. Hatala

The Human Side of Just-In-Time, by Charlene Adair-Heely

The Team Approach to Quality, by Karl A. Shilliff and Paul J. Motiska

On Service Quality

TQM for Sales and Marketing Management, by James Cortada

The Quality Sales Leadership: System for Today's Financial Executive, by Niki Nicastro McCuistion and Jeffrey N. Senne

Quality Dynamics for the Service Industry, by W.F. Drewes

Quality Service Pays, by Henry L. Lefevre

Deming's 14 Points Applied to Service, by A.C. Rosander

Measuring Customer Satisfaction: Development and Use of Questionnaires, by Bob E. Hayes

BIBLIOGRAPHY

Byham, William C., and Jeff Cox. *Zapp! The Lightning of Empowerment: How to Improve Productivity, Quality and Employee Satisfaction.* New York: Harmony Books, 1988.

Covey, Stephen R. *The 7 Habits of Highly Effective People: Powerful Lessons in Personal Change.* New York: Simon and Schuster, 1990.

Crosby, Philip B. *Quality Is Free: The Art of Making Quality Certain.* New York: Penguin Group, 1980.

Deming, W. Edwards. *Out of the Crisis.* Massachusetts: The Massachusetts Institute of Technology, 1990.

Haefner, Joe, Shelly Hornback, Thea Hefty and Andrea Hughes. "7 Step Improvement Process: Overview Document." Madison: CUNA Service Group, 1993.

Harrington, H. James. *Business Process Improvement: The Breakthrough Strategy for Total Quality, Productivity, and Competitiveness.* McGraw-Hill, Inc., 1991.

Ishikawa, Kaoru. *What Is Total Quality Control? The Japanese Way.* New Jersey: Prentice-Hall Inc., 1985.

Juran, J.M. *Juran on Leadership for Quality: An Executive Handbook.* New York: The Free Press, 1989.

Juran, J.M. *Juran on Planning for Quality.* New York: The Free Press, 1988.

Juran, J.M. *Juran on Quality by Design: The New Steps for Planning Quality into Goods and Services.* New York: The Free Press, 1992.

Juran, J.M., Frank M. Gryna, Jr., and R.S. Bingham, Jr. *Quality Control Handbook.* McGraw-Hill, Inc., 1979.

McCuistion, Niki Nicastro, and Jeffrey N. Senne. *The Quality Sales Leadership: System for Today's Financial Executive.* Dearborn Financial Publishing, Inc., 1993.

Scholtes, Peter R. *The Team Handbook.* Madison: Joiner Associates, 1988.

Senge, Peter M. *The Fifth Discipline: The Art and Practice of the Learning Organization.* New York: Doubleday, 1990.

Walton, Mary. *The Deming Management Method.* New York: The Putnam Publishing Group, 1986.

EVALUATION SHEET

To gauge how useful this manual is to credit unions, we need your evaluation and comments. Your frank appraisal will help us in revising future editions of *Total Quality Management: A Credit Union Reader,* and in developing supplementary materials.

After you read the manual, please take a moment to fill out and return this evaluation form.

Please rate *Total Quality Management: A Credit Union Reader* by indicating whether you agree or disagree with the following statements:

AGREE   **DISAGREE**

_____   _____   1. The manual provides a basic understanding of total quality management as it relates to credit unions.

_____   _____   2. The content is thorough and is presented in a way that is easy to understand.

_____   _____   3. The material is applicable to current needs within your credit union.

Comments or suggestions for improving this manual:

_____
_____

What other materials would you find useful concerning TQM? Please list topics that you would like to see covered, or formats (print, video, audiotape, other) that would be used in your credit union:

_____
_____

Please tear out this sheet, fold and seal, and return to the address shown on the back. Thank you!

CUNA & Affiliates
Human Resource Development Department
Attention: Educational Materials
P.O. Box 431
Madison, WI 53701-0431